hintz blowsy blooms inspiring conversa
anglaise old gold frames quilted fabric banksias old books
ried hydrangeas weddings Woollahra in autumn scratched &
rquetry Willow pattern swimming at La Fontelina in summer
w hats tablecloths still-life paintings Persian rugs split cane
the barge to Straddie old plaster moulding verandahs Art
ad autobiographies old portrait paintings lattice junk shops
unday lunch in the garden the scent of sweet peas antiques
kes floating in the ocean finding things unexpectedly baking
s Harry's painted rocks flower paintings baskets embroidery
jam herbs in vases on the kitchen bench odd numbers raw
even spacing Sundays with my boys discoveries garden paths
dmade things kisses and cuddles honesty Christmas morning
ngles espadrilles indigo good-luck charms scrapbooks and
ards Simon and Garfunkel wild flowers tassels and tiebacks
ed edges antique armoires as linen cupboards wild lilies in
g breakfast outside hessian parchment starting a new year
osgrain old busts originality hat blocks and boxes to-do lists
-you cards family and friends.

Magic is
something
you make

{Unknown}

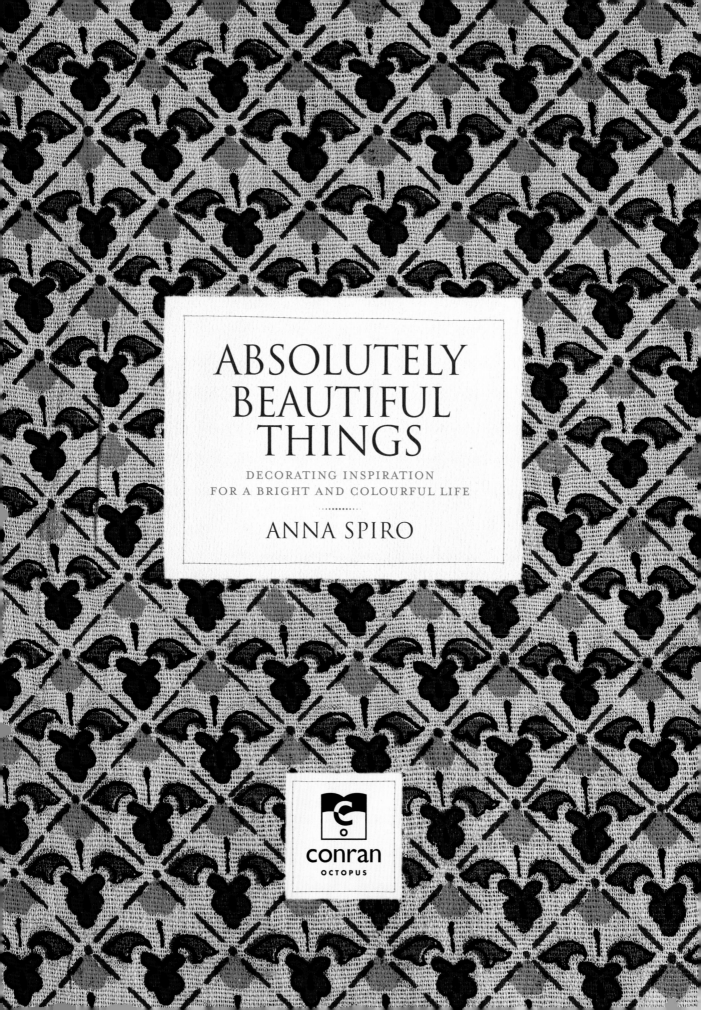

ABSOLUTELY BEAUTIFUL THINGS

DECORATING INSPIRATION
FOR A BRIGHT AND COLOURFUL LIFE

· · · · · · ·

ANNA SPIRO

conran
OCTOPUS

For Mum, Grandma & Lel,
I live every single day of my
life inspired and motivated by
everything you have taught me.

For Dad, thank you for
teaching me that I must live
my life with uncompromising
integrity.

And for Brad, Harry & Max,
because you are my everything,
and my life wouldn't be
worth living without you.

I love you all so very much.

CONTENTS

My look

Nothing in my world matches and everything in my world clashes. I am confident enough with my own style to only run with things I love — things like a ticking sofa, a collection of floral, striped and geometric cushions, a floral armchair, a kilim-upholstered ottoman, an antique round table and a colourful lamp. Certainly a mismatched collection of things and yet somehow it all works. As far as I'm concerned, there's no such thing as a decorating rule book — and if there were, I'd be all for breaking the rules. To create a look that is unique and interesting, that's what it's all about.

I believe in the concept of the more you layer the better. I'm a maximalist, not a minimalist. It's important to collect things over time — and only things you love or that have meaning to you — and let your home gradually evolve; that way you come to notice common factors or special threads that bind everything together. It might be a certain colour that creeps into everything, or a certain shape. Mix expensive with inexpensive, modern with antique; timber with metal; objects of different heights; the rough with the refined. The most important thing is to know what you love and know what you don't love. Once you have that sorted, you can do anything.

In my family home and the houses I design, I always endeavour to create happy, interesting, layered and uplifting spaces. That means mixing everything: colour and pattern, old and new, square and round, quirky and conservative. It is by no means a perfect, textbook decorating style (in fact, some people might be horrified by it), but it's the imperfections and the surprises that make a space interesting, appropriate and so special and unique for the people living there.

It's taken me a long time to understand how, and why, I do some of the things I do — it's not something that just happened overnight. I've always loved to share knowledge, and part of the reason I've written this book is to be able to pass along ideas, thoughts and information I've picked up over the years. It's information I've been given, have gleaned from elsewhere or have worked out along the way. The main thing I've learnt, though, is that, at its best, your home should be a true reflection of you — I hope, through this book, I help you achieve this.

"When to luv"

THINGS

OBERTO GILI HOME SWEET HOME

HABITUALLY CHIC Creativity at Work HEATHER CLAWSON

BLACK WHITE (and a bit in between) CELERIE KEMBLE

Yves Saint Laurent
David Teboul

THINGS I LOVE MEGAN MORTON

INSPIRATION
CONRAN
STAFFORD CLIFF

part 01

· · · · · · · · · ·

{ DEVELOPING MY LOOK }

Generations of women in my family
have been passionate about art, design
and colour. Growing up in such a world
has had a strong influence on me and my
life as a designer.

My sense of style

It has only been in the last few years that I have truly developed my own sense of style. At about the age of thirty, I started to establish some sense of all the different things and looks I loved, and to understand how to bring them all together beautifully and in a balanced way within a space. I've had to evaluate my influences and try different things before I've had the confidence to run with what I really love.

I have always been very wary of heading full steam ahead with one particular theme, such as the Balinese look, the Hamptons look or the Hollywood Regency look – going wholeheartedly into any one of these means the scheme eventually dates. Instead, I have always tried to throw in a bit of every style so that the look will stand the test of time. To prevent it getting tired or needing a major and expensive overhaul after a few years, this style of decorating can evolve and be updated along the way. A few years ago, I arrived at a place when I just thought, 'This is what I love, this is what I want, and this is what I will do.' I have always used lots of bright colours in an eclectic way, but believe my style has now matured into a more 'collected' style of brights as accents mixed with antiques, modern and vintage art, textiles and texture, which can be found in the likes of timber, glass and ceramics.

Over the years, like many designers, I have used my own home and my shop as test labs for experimenting with different looks, styles and fabric combinations. There have been a few times when things weren't quite right, but these moments were the stepping stones I needed, to know and understand what worked and what didn't.

For instance, a number of years ago I selected a bright, multi-coloured striped linen fabric to upholster a sofa for our lounge room at home. From the moment it was delivered, I absolutely hated it. It was a big mistake and consequently didn't hang around for too long. It was too bold and took away from everything else in the room. The best upholstery fabric for a sofa is plain or a ticking or something with a very small pattern. That way, you can layer the bold, bright stripes and floral fabrics onto it with cushions. If you tire of the cushions, they can easily be changed.

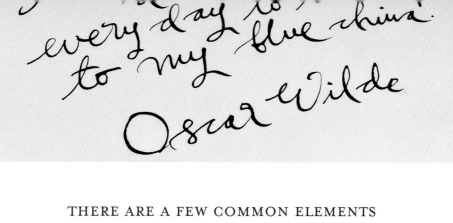

...every day to... to my blue china.

Oscar Wilde

THERE ARE A FEW COMMON ELEMENTS
– IN EVERY ROOM I CREATE –

~

Antique furniture, such as a table, sideboard or chest
of drawers, to ground the colourful fabrics I use.

~

A mix of fabrics in different patterns and colours.

~

A specific underlying colour that will pull everything together.

~

A surprise element, such as a vibrantly patterned lampshade
or a quirky vintage piece of furniture or even a collection
of Staffordshire dogs displayed in a vignette on a table.
It's all about the unexpected.

~

A mix of expensive and inexpensive pieces. For example,
a cushion collection looks wonderful when you throw a cheap
ready-made cushion into the mix or include a vintage fabric.
This makes it look less contrived and a little more effortless.

~

White painted walls as a backdrop for the entire mismatch.
That way, there's some cohesiveness to the room.

~

A collection of art which is added to over the years and
which may comprise a mix of valuable pieces and paintings
created by children.

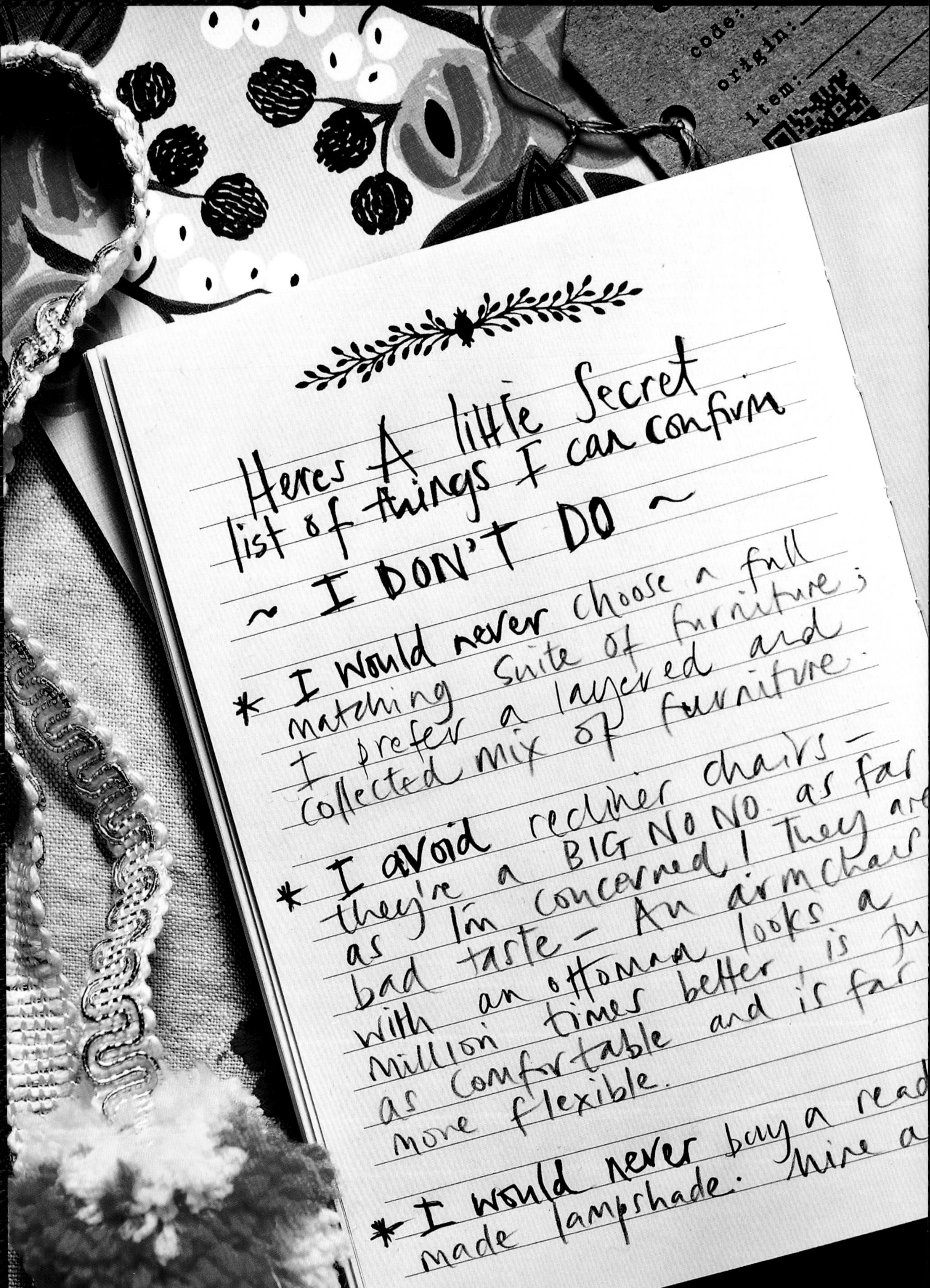

code:
origin:
item:

Heres A little Secret.
list of things I can confirm
~ I DON'T DO ~

* I would never choose a full
matching Suite of furniture;
I prefer a layered and
collected mix of furniture.

* I avoid recliner chairs—
they're a BIG NO NO as far
as I'm concerned! They are
bad taste— An armchair
with an ottoman looks a
million times better is ju
as comfortable and is far
more flexible.

* I would never buy a read
made lampshade. hire a

...ways custom made. Apart from
...king things to be handmade
...nd of high quality, ready-
...made lampshades are never
...quite the right dimensions.

* I never use Dacron cushion
inserts. I prefer pure feather
or a mix of feather with down,
foam or fibre. A cheap
synthetic cushion flattens in
minutes. You can spend around
$25 and get a feather mix
that lasts 10-15 years.

* I don't like or ever suggest
leather sofas. Thats my personal
preference, although I wouldn't
say no to an old and worn
French leather chair.

I grew up surrounded by blue and white. Not just a bit here and there. I am the daughter of a blue and white addict. From old blue and white ginger jars to batik textiles, willow patterned plates and upholstery fabrics, Mum has always decorated her home with different hues of blue. From the deepest indigo to the palest milky blue, and always set against simple, fresh white and lots of beautiful dark timber antiques. With the choice of this classic colour combination, her house never falls victim to trends, and looks as fresh as the day she started decorating it. Having lived with so much blue and white as a child, I vowed in my early twenties I would never do the 'blue and white thing'. I tried to escape it; I wanted to have my own look. But no matter how hard I tried to avoid it, I seemed to include a little bit of blue and white in most projects.

It's as if I instantly feel at home now when I see it. But the way I mix blue and white with bright colour is my way of blending my past and my present, what I grew up with and what I love today. The end result is a classic look with a refreshing, youthful facelift.

The process

Walking into a client's home for the first time, I am embarking on an adventure of discovery. I think of myself as an explorer looking for treasure, taking note of everything in the house. In my head I establish two lists. The first covers the furniture and objects that can remain in the house as-is or which may need re-covering or repainting. These are what I refer to as 'the key pieces of greatness'. The second list contains the items that need to be replaced. It's almost like sorting the washing into piles.

I also look for hints of what the client likes and dislikes. It could be colours in an artwork or in a rug, and that will be the kernel of inspiration I use as a starting point for creating the whole look.

Pulling together a concept, I start with the collection of fabrics. I am passionate about them — their patterns, colours and textures are a very important element in the rooms I design. Once I establish the trophy fabric, the multicoloured pièce de résistance of the entire scheme and something I'll talk more about later, it's a matter of deciding the patterned and coloured fabrics that work with this. Once that all comes together, I select the sofa and armchair styles, the lamps and other furniture pieces required.

I recently put a scheme together for a client with a collection of old blue and white china. Because of that, I created a blue and white colour scheme, with layers of pink, green, yellow and orange. The idea was to have white walls, sisal rugs on her timber floors, sofas and armchairs re-covered in navy and white plain and ticking fabrics, and patterned fabrics for cushions and lampshades. When she arrived at my studio to hear my ideas, she was surprised by all the blue and white, and was expecting more green. Later, she rang to say when she looked around at home, she realised she really did love blue and white, and we continued with my ideas. It's worth having another pair of eyes to help you see the things you own which you may have been disregarding for years.

How I started

My first part-time job, at the age of 16, was waiting tables at a Chinese restaurant near home. But it was my second job, a year later, that turned out to be one of the greatest things that has ever happened to me.

I vividly remember a phone conversation my mother had with my grandmother Ellie Spiro in September, 1994, a few months before I left school. She had just heard that her friend and renowned Brisbane interior decorator John Black needed a new assistant in his studio. As I had no solid plans for the future, other than the possibility of heading to university to do an arts degree, this exciting opportunity couldn't have come at a better time.

I was a particularly shy girl and remember nervously, yet with anticipation, visiting John Black in his studio with my mother and grandmother in tow for an informal job interview. Wearing a floor-length summer dress, I innocently floated into his office as quiet as a mouse yet as hopeful as a sailor lost at sea.

In all reality, why would anyone want to employ a fresh-faced young girl with no training and experience? However, thanks to my grandmother's incredible zeal, I was fortunate enough to get the job.

As I needed to finish off my final school year, my grandmother put her hand up to temporarily fill the position, working for John until I could start in the December. I really have no idea where I would be today without her help, encouragement, support and belief in me. To think that at the age of sixty-seven, she put her life on hold to go to work so the job could be mine when I finished school humbles me no end.

December rolled in and as all my friends celebrated the end of school, I started working in the job that took me by the hand and has never let me go. The stars aligned for me that summer. The most important thing is I took that special opportunity and ran with it, and John taught me so much. I was focused and ambitious and didn't ever give up. I kept going because that is what my family has taught me to do. I had to do everything in my power to make my grandmother proud and happy that she took that leap of faith for me all those years ago.

As all my friends celebrated the end of school, I started working in the job that took me by the hand and has never let me go.

Wearing a floor-length summer dress, I innocently floated into his office as quiet as a mouse yet as hopeful as a sailor lost at sea.

The early days

After working for John Black for almost six years, he asked me to go into partnership with him. We opened Black & Spiro in 2001 in Hamel, an art deco building in the middle of New Farm, and we're still there today. It belongs to my mother's close friend Diana Favell, her husband Paul and her brother and sister-in-law Frank and Lora Calvisi. At the time, it had suffered rough tenants for years and was in dire need of refurbishment. Even in its derelict state, I admired it and was thrilled when the Favells and Calvisis said we could move in, and renovated it for us. I'm in love with Hamel. I hope we can stay within her pretty walls and divine ceilings for a very long time. We've been through a lot together!!

When we started, New Farm was on the cusp of becoming an inner-city hot spot. Our decorating work has always been the backbone of the business, with the retail side being slow and therefore very stressful in those early days. I didn't want it to get the better of me because I knew I could make it work if I worked hard enough at it. Early on, I worried about cash flow and where the next job would be coming from. I've always thought of the business as a large engine that I continuously have to inject with lots of fuel, the fuel being me. There was also the stress of clients loving the schemes I would put together but then not understanding how much custom-made things cost. I would put my whole creative spirit into coming up with something beautiful for a house only to be disappointed when we got a no-go after the client received the price. If I'm honest, it's still difficult to deal with people's expectations. However, the many tears I shed, the late nights, early mornings, extremely hard work and unrelenting stress did eventually pay off.

About a year after we opened Black & Spiro, James Marks (who then owned the fabric agency, Wardlaw, and these days is managing director of Radford Furnishings) told me great success is not necessarily about being in the best retail position on the busiest street. It's about being in a boutique position and finding something you become a leader in. Those words would ring in my ears for the next ten years, and made me think about what I was doing and what I needed to do to become successful. I needed to find a look, an idea, a style of my own. If it was good, people would come. That's what I did, and I look back and realise that even though I fell into my blog, it was the vehicle that drove me on my journey. Even though Black & Spiro was situated in a beautiful building in the middle of busy, trendy New Farm, it has never had a passing trade to rely on. I had to shout out about it and make it a place like no other, with absolutely beautiful things that people from all over would come to, be inspired by and want a piece of.

VOGUE FIRST CLASS

e identity
...tner make their mark on an old country
...eate a bolthole from the Big Apple.
...PETE BERNDO

NICOLE BENTLEY

Blogging

I first stumbled across blogs when I Google-searched a particular decorating subject back in 2005. The search brought up an article written by Courtney Barnes. The page had the header 'style court'. I had no idea what this document was, but eventually after a bit of Googling, the definition of 'blogs' that came up was: 'A website on which an individual or group of users record opinions, information, etc. on a regular basis.' I was so curious and excited to find all of this wonderful information and inspiration. (It seems so odd now that only a short time ago it was such a mystery, when now everyone knows what a blog is, and has probably even tried writing one.) Scrolling back through Courtney's entire blog, I was hooked, started following her, and a few months later she inspired me to start my own blog, Absolutely Beautiful Things.

That was in 2006. The idea was that Absolutely Beautiful Things would work as a record of my work and my daily thoughts and inspirations. It's incredible that it would eventually be read by thousands of people every day. In sharing thoughts of my life, I have continually been surprised that my experiences have become a source of inspiration to others. Through the blog, I have made connections with like-minded people around the world. As with Instagram, it is a direct connection with creative people and a wonderfully encouraging community.

Strangely enough, my blog helped me understand what I was good at. Looking back at some of the work I had posted, I started to see that I did have my own particular style. The blog also gave me great confidence. When I posted pictures of particular projects of mine, or little snippets of things I had created in the shop, my readers would encourage me and leave wonderful comments about things they loved. Without the encouragement and support of my readers, I wouldn't be where I am today.

THE NEW YORKER

ANNA SPIRO

PORTER'S
ORIGINAL
PAINTS

SPECIALITY FINISHES   PAPER   WIDE BOARD TIMBER FLOORING

The three women in my life

It's important for me to acknowledge my mother and grandmothers. With their strong style influences and creative nurturing, they have exposed me to a wonderful array of experiences which have shaped the way I think.

Ellie Spiro, whom we affectionately call Lel, has unmistakable style. Her aunt Lyn James was a couture fashion designer in 1940s Brisbane. Lel worked with Aunty Lyn for years, helping her design and make the most exquisite gowns. Through this, she honed her eye for fabric, colour combinations and quality. When I was little, she would make me dresses from the most heavenly fabrics and trims. Her eye for quality is unerring and her love of beautiful handmade things has been passed on to our entire family. I am inspired by the way she pulls together an outfit. At the age of eighty-six, she wears flat brown brogues with tailored tweed pants, a white tee and a Tom Binns neon necklace. There's nobody else like her and I am in awe of her confident, offbeat, yet cohesive personal style.

My mother's mother, Grandma, is a creative genius, and has always immersed herself in a diverse range of projects such as making divine couture hats for the different occasions of her life. Her skill at designing and making her own dresses and outfits, including my mother's wedding dress, is something I wish I had inherited. She is an artist and, at ninety-eight, still paints in her painting room which is filled with easels, paintbrushes, canvases, failed (in her opinion) paintings and vintage frames. The room used to be my mother's bedroom and is still wallpapered in the black and white ticking wallpaper she chose when she was fifteen. Always trying to be thrifty and thinking she could do things better than anyone else, my grandmother hung the wallpaper herself and, despite showing its age with a few tears here and there, it's as in fashion today as it was almost fifty years ago.

As I walk through her timber cottage on the front block of my grandfather's family estate, I admire her gallery of paintings, hung high and low on every wall. She mostly paints pretty still-life scenes, usually of a vignette using an array of her collected objects and, almost always, one of her flower arrangements. Her love of art and colour rubbed off on me, maybe because she took me to the art gallery as much as she could when I was little, or perhaps it was the time we spent watering her cherished pink azaleas, or propagating orchids and African violets in her greenhouse. What I now realise is the hours we spent together included some of the most valuable – most precious – lessons of my life: lessons on colour, fabric, flowers, drawing, sewing, cooking and style.

My mother taught me there is nowhere more important than home. Home is where we entertain, relax, celebrate, play, hide, nurture our children, create memories and rejuvenate our souls. It is a reflection of all that we are and all that we love. When I close my eyes and think about my life and what is important to me, one of my first images is of my mother, happily cooking in her kitchen for her beloved family. And I think about us sitting at the dinner table, set with her favourite tablecloth, plates and napkins, beautiful candles she has collected, and fresh flowers from her garden.

Rummaging through antique stores with Mum and Grandma helped me gain knowledge of what to look for in the perfect piece of

furniture. They didn't teach me, but shaped my mind by the way they'd talk. I'd pick up on what they thought was nice, or not nice. It was the experience of spending time with them, seeing what they liked, and listening to what they talked about. I try to do the same with my boys. I think parents often underestimate how much their children take in.

I have written many blog posts on the profound influence my mother has had on my appreciation for beautiful things. She encourages me to surround myself with things with meaning: antiques, treasures from holidays and special handcrafted pieces. Mum has an innate sense of style and, just as importantly, the confidence to trust her instinct. It's allowed her to run with her heart, to do exactly what she thinks, rather than copying a look or style.

With these three extraordinary women in my life, it was inevitable that I would end up working in a creative industry surrounded by the things they had been teaching me about since I was a little girl — colour, pattern, collecting, fabric and beauty.

*It's largely because
of my mother that I've learnt to
think outside the square
and to embrace a look that
is absolutely my own.*

Be a neo-traditionalist.
Bring back into your life today
the ways and traditions of your
family's past.

Inspired by the past

I believe in tradition. In following thoughts, actions, ideas and tastes passed down from the older generations. Family traditions evoke memories of special places and times. By fostering them, you draw inspiration from your family's past. It might be that your grandmother collected a particular brand of china and so you collect the same set. You may want to hang the plates on your kitchen wall, so that every time you look at them you are reminded of her. By incorporating things from our family's past into our lives today, we are setting a standard and a unique style in which to live our lives.

American interior designer Sister Parish's quote, 'Even the simplest wicker basket can become priceless when it is loved and cared for through the generations of a family', resonates with me. For as long as I can remember, my mother has carted her goods and chattels from our beach house in wicker baskets, big and small, much to my father's annoyance. He insisted they were a pain to pack in the car. She'd traipse to the beach, three children in tow, a beach umbrella under one arm and a basket over the other, filled with sunscreen, magazines, buckets and spades, towels, hats, drinks and enough spare change for the ice cream man. Her obsession with baskets has rubbed off on me and I find myself picking up old ones, partly because I find them beautiful but, more importantly, they remind me of happy times. With my growing collection and my mother's, I hope my children are prepared for the mountain of baskets they will inherit!

Another collector was Topsy, my cousin's grandmother, who would gather shells near the family beach house. When Topsy passed away, my cousin Ben kept some of the shells. They now sit in a bowl at his house, as a reminder of time spent with her. This shell-collecting tradition will be shared by Ben with his own children on the same beach he and his grandmother walked along almost thirty years ago.

*Sometimes
it can be easy to overlook
simple, quiet pleasures,
yet the memory of them
can linger, quite beautifully
through generations.*

Simple pleasures

Material ingredients are necessary for building and creating a beautiful home for your family to live in, but it is very important to understand that, without the very simple pleasures which life has to offer, no house could ever be a home. My mother always tried to instil in my brothers and me an appreciation for simple pleasures. Find happiness, excitement and pure joy in the most basic, no-frills experiences and objects life has to offer. For example, be excited about the flowers growing in your garden which you can go out and cut and arrange in a vase for your dining table; revel in the sense of achievement from building a fire in your fireplace in the winter, and then enjoy sitting in front of it roasting marshmallows with your family. Keep an open mind, be observant and aware of special little treasures along your way and don't let a simple pleasure pass you by.

Gardening & flowers

When I was a little girl we lived in an old Queenslander with
a beautiful garden, which my mother took great pride in. She
grew daisies and sweet peas, iceberg and standard roses, calendulas,
primulas and cinerarias. My friend and I used to pick flowers and
sell them from a stall in front of our house. That garden offered me
my first opportunity for entrepreneurship and was the inspiration
for my wallpaper collection. Many of the colour palettes that form the
basis of my designs have been inspired by nature, especially the beauty
of flowers. In nature, we have blue skies, green trees, yellow, orange
and pink flowers, brown soil – the perfect colour palette for a room.

These days I live in an old Queenslander with my husband
Brad and two children. I, too, have a large garden, which we plant
seasonally with favourite things like poppies, dahlias, sweet peas,
zinnias and hollyhocks. I love being able to head out into our garden
to cut bunches of flowers to place on tables and mantelpieces.

If you don't have lots of flowering plants in your garden, green
branches look just as effective. Things like travellers palm, ginger
leaves, frangipani branches, banksia, apple blossom foliage and even
palm tree seed husks look fabulous and sculptural. Anything bushy
or green or dried can look great arranged in a vase, jug or jar.

On install day at my clients' houses, I try to find some green
things in their garden to arrange into vases. By showing them how
great something from their garden can look, I'm encouraging them
to use what they have. You don't always have to buy flowers. Discover
what you have in your own garden. You might be surprised!

*I love being able to head
out into our garden to cut
bunches of flowers to place
on tables and mantelpieces.*

A seashell,
a bird's nest,
some flowers

This morning I went for one
of my long morning walks on the beach.
Along the way I found three very beautiful
things. A seashell, a little bird's nest
perfectly rounded and crafted and some
very pretty dune flowers. I can't explain
to you the joy these beautiful natural
objects gave me.

by Tess McCabe

part 02

· · · · · · · · · · ·

{ ESTABLISHING YOUR SENSE OF STYLE }

Developing your own sense of style
is a matter of looking around you, and
discovering what you love — and don't love
— and finding what's right for you.
In this section, I help you learn
to trust your instincts.

Recognising your 'special thread'

Over the years, through reading magazines, books and blogs, I have spent a lot of time observing tastemakers and stylish people. Everyone I admire and consider to have great style does so with outward thinking. In simple terms, stylish people always think and act outside the box. Their look seems so different yet perfectly and effortlessly thrown together. It is important to realise their look is unique. We should be inspired by such people, not copy them slavishly.

Pluck up some courage and go out on a limb with a look you love and believe in. Now, please don't think this is something you can do overnight. It takes time for the thread to form. You have to gather your ideas, thoughts, pieces and collections over time in order for your look to have depth. Don't be discouraged if you make a wrong decision — we all do. Just get back on that horse and try again. It will all fall into place in the end. It always does.

To understand and own your unique sense of style, it's important to be aware of your 'style roots', who you are and who, and what, has influenced you. Whether it's the times your grandparents took you to the art gallery, the trips to a local decorating shop with your mum or the wallpaper you had in your bedroom, don't try to escape the style influences you had as a child. Embrace them and incorporate them into your home and life. Without these influences there wouldn't be a starting point. By mixing them with new ideas, you are creating a look that can only be yours.

Working out what you like

Making a judgment on something for your home should be your own decision. Although it's nice to get advice from a friend, it's best not to let them persuade you to do something that suits them, but not necessarily you. What one person loves another person loathes. Make a decision because you love it, not because your friend or neighbour loves it. When establishing your own look, it's important to embrace the concept of 'Who cares what anyone else thinks?' If you decorate with things you love and collect things from your travels to mix in with existing pieces and objects, your personality will shine through and your home will reflect this.

Sometimes I make unconscious decisions; I have no idea why, the idea just comes to me, and I run with it. These are the Bermuda Triangle sections of my mind and it's impossible for me to try to explain them. Over the years, I have discovered that if I think it will work, it will. This confidence comes with experience. Learning to trust your instincts does take some time. Some people think too hard about style choices. If you like something, do it. If you don't, then find an alternative. Sometimes I have to sleep on a decision and often I've asked the girls to order a fabric for a particular purpose and arrive into the office the next morning and ask them to cancel it and order another one instead. They have become quite accustomed to this little habit of mine and often don't order the first one I decide on until I've slept on it, and then either told them it's okay or to change it. The most harebrained, unplanned ideas are often the best.

You too must learn to trust your instincts. Just run with an idea, even if you don't quite know how it will look in the end. If you really love something, you will find a way of making it work. Often obsessing over something can cause confusion, and will hinder any decisions. Have confidence in yourself and just do it!

wind in the willows

The relaxed, poetic silhouettes that dominate this season's offerings come together with billowing layers and whimsical details

Window, Grand Hotel, Vittel, 1970

i love to th moo

Collect your thoughts

When you are able to organise your thoughts, your natural style will start to shine through. The pieces of the thread will start to form and you will begin to understand what you truly love and truly dislike. Here are some things I use to help gather my thoughts and ideas.

I always have a camera with me (usually my phone) to record anything that catches my eye. It might be a fabulous piece I have stumbled across or an interesting colour palette or graphic that strikes a chord. Keep these images for reference and you will see some common elements start to emerge.

All the walls in my design studio are a very pale icing pink – Dulux Marshmallow Magic quarter strength. This lovely floaty colour inspires wonderful creative thoughts, and it is the perfect soft background to washi tape magazine tear sheets to. Amazingly, pale pink goes with everything, so it really is the perfect colour for my studio. Coloured washi tape adds a fun, attractive and informal scrapbook effect. (I can't bring myself to tear apart my treasured magazines, so I either photocopy the images or buy two copies so that one can be torn up and the other kept in perfect condition.)

If you prefer a more structured inspiration board, get a large corkboard made to your desired size by a cabinet-maker and have it covered in fabric. Natural coloured linen works well, as it doesn't interfere with the bits of inspiration you pin on top.

Some kind
of wonderful

Bourne identity

N° 5

THE AVERAGE GIRL

By CECIL H. S. WILLSON, M.A.

IN many years, experience of the education and training for life of girls as well as boys, I have naturally been frequently brought into contact with "the average girl." It has often been brought home to me forcibly in school life that there are numbers of girls of fifteen years and upwards who are beginning to ask anxiously though secretly a similar question to that which St. Peter put to our Lord about the beloved disciple: "Lord, and what shall this woman do?"

The average girl begins to take serious stock of her position in the life of the school and in the larger life going on around her. It begins to dawn more forcibly upon her that she is, after all, not very rich and not very poor, not very clever and not very stupid, not very popular but not disliked. It is well to be sure at the outset that the dangers attaching to the girl with two talents are quite as great as, though differing from, the dangers that await the girl with five talents and the girl with only one.

It is so fatally easy for this average girl to argue to herself that after all not very much can be expected from her in most of the departments of school life, and this so often leads to a slackening of effort and a failure to live up to the best she is really capable of in work and games. A little quiet talk and time for quiet thought will often make such girls realise that they are missing the whole point of the Parable of the Talents by dwelling morbidly on the number of talents granted and not the use made of them.

There are so many spheres of activity and helpfulness in modern school life in which the girl of only one talent can make good use of it. If she does not shine in the ordinary school work and games, she may have an artistic eye, and can render invaluable help in the tasteful decoration of the classroom with pictures and flowers. She may have a gift for tidiness which will find full scope in the cloakroom and bring blessings on her head from harassed mistresses. She may have just a sweet natural disposition, finest of all, which takes no pleasure in idle school gossip, and still tries to believe the best of everybody.

There are indeed few who do not possess one talent to exercise to the full for the good of the school and the glory of God. The vital thing to remember is that there is no such thing as unimportant work in the Great Taskmaster's eye, either at school or in the world. The fourth-form girl who is struggling away conscientiously at her French, or the insignificant junior doing her best in the Hockey House Tie is every bit as important in the real scheme of things as the Senior Prefect or the Games Captain. In every sphere of life it is the effort and the intention combined with thoroughness which really count, and not the result. Results, whether in examinations or games, are largely an affair of the judgment of men, but "when time and God give judgment" the work of an efficient and conscientious plumber, when found, will be of as great importance as that of a Prime Minster.

We have only to go back to the Carpenter's Shop at Nazareth to realise how Jesus made this profoundly true for all time. How often in later years when He was using those beautiful images of the "yokes and ploughs" in His talks to the people, must His thoughts have turned wistfully to the earlier peaceful years when He made them with Joseph! Of one thing we may be certain, and that is that those yokes and ploughs were wrought conscientiously, efficiently and lovingly. In school life it is the spirit which quickeneth

ston says. "It's
f the window."
erston has had
, then layered
etween playful
a 16th-century
g that Ferjani
oks are piled
re decoration in

Indian
summer

Eclectic, colourful, crazy ... The modern gypsy's style is every bit as exoti

I also love...

to organise my inspiration and ideas into ring binder folders stored on shelves in my studio. Here I keep images of furniture details, curtain styles, cabinetry profiles and all sorts of specific detailed images. These are an essential resource, and I look to them almost every day when putting rooms together. If you are more tech-savvy, use your iPad and create folders in your picture files to store your images appropriately or, as so many people do, use Pinterest.

On a practical level, Pinterest is a great way to catalogue your photos in specific themes. You can catalogue your dream life — what to wear, where to travel to, how you'd like your house to be. With Pinterest, information can be stored in one practical easy-to-use place, and you're able to reference things you like. There are so many pretty pictures in the world!

Start a blog to post pictures of things you love and write down your thoughts and ideas. You may get followers, you may not, but that's not the point — it will remain as a record for you to look back upon years down the track.

Once you start to bring together your ideas, you will start to see a common thread running through your pictures, whether it be a certain colour combination, a furniture style or particular piece, or patterns and textures that you always seem to come back to. These are the building blocks you can use to start piecing together your own look and style for your home.

A CORRECT AND DELICATE MIND

LINDA MARRINON'S RECENT SCULPTURE
CHRIS MCAULIFFE

A collection of French 19th-c. oans is a family room focal point. French 19th-c. étagère. Armchairs in Rogers & Goffigon linen slipcovers. French 19th-c. doors, Chateau Domingue. Dhurrie, Carol Piper Rugs. OPPOSITE: Coffee table, floor lamp, and French 19th-c. banquette, Jane Moore Interiors. Shades in Rogers & Goffigon linen. OPENING PAGES: Vintage sofa and chairs in Boussac cottons. Curtains in Great Plains linen. Mirror from French 18th-c. panel. Floor lamps, Circa Lighting. Vintage sconces.

gold and pearl embroidered dress with organza ruff, made to order, by **Alexander McQueen**

Shopping at home

This is the very best place to start when you are redecorating. Often you can underestimate what you already have, so take a metaphorical step back and reassess the pieces you own. Move things around, or pull out those items you may have stored away in a cupboard or in the back shed. Using this approach can be a breath of fresh air throughout your home. A small table or chest of drawers may just need an update with a coat of paint. The shape of your sofa might still work well but would look totally different re-covered in new fabric. Alternatively, have it professionally cleaned and inject some colour with some new cushions. Maybe you have a vast collection of jugs or platters hidden away in a top cupboard that might look wonderful displayed on top of an armoire or hung on the wall in your kitchen. You will be so surprised at what a bit of thought and a fresh eye can do to uplift and reinvigorate the rooms within your home. If you shake things up a little, you will provide some much-needed spark.
I recently redecorated a room at home on a tight budget using lots of old pieces of furniture I already owned. The only new things I added were some cushions, a lamp with a gorgeous patterned lampshade, a sisal rug and a couple of paintings. All the other pieces, such as the sofas, the chest of drawers, the sofa table and armchair, were things I already had. The room now looks like a completely different space as a result of the few new additions and new layout.

A modern Saarinen marble topped table in a breakfast room with antique bentwood dining chairs is a fabulous look. So, too, are Hans Wegner Wishbone chairs around an antique table. The combination throws the room into an unpredictable, exciting space. I recently did some work in a house with the best art collection I had seen. The art and antique furniture gave the house the most amazing ambience but the absolute success came from the few modern and inexpensive pieces thrown into the mix, such as the yellow IKEA locker-style cabinet underneath a divine abstract painting in a hallway. The contrast of modern and old, inexpensive and expensive is something that will create a wonderful, eclectic and purely individual style in your home.

Buy once. Buy well.

Buy well from the start

Instead of wasting money on of-the-moment items that will most likely be discarded down the track, it's important to buy good pieces in the first place. This technique will actually save you money in the long run, even though the initial outlay may be more. Don't buy all your pieces from stores such as IKEA or Freedom, but try to break it up a bit. Buy some things from chain stores, others from antique and vintage stores as well as from flea markets and maybe, if your budget allows, a few custom-made pieces from your local decorator. Perhaps a hand-embroidered textile here, a hand-painted treasure there. This will ensure an individual, layered and very stylish result, and possibly one that hasn't emptied your bank account!

Buy things from your heart. If you run with what you love, you will eventually see that the pieces all tie in together to form that collected look I love. Your house is a self-portrait of you, and so it should be. The greatest compliment you can receive is if someone walks in and says, 'This house is so you.'

When starting to furnish your home, begin with one room and move through the rest of the house in stages. That way, you can set your mind and concentrate on one area rather than get confused and overwhelmed about the different pieces you need to find for all the rooms of your home. That's not to say, though, if you happen to come across something you love that might work somewhere else in the house, you shouldn't buy it. If you love it, you'll make it work!

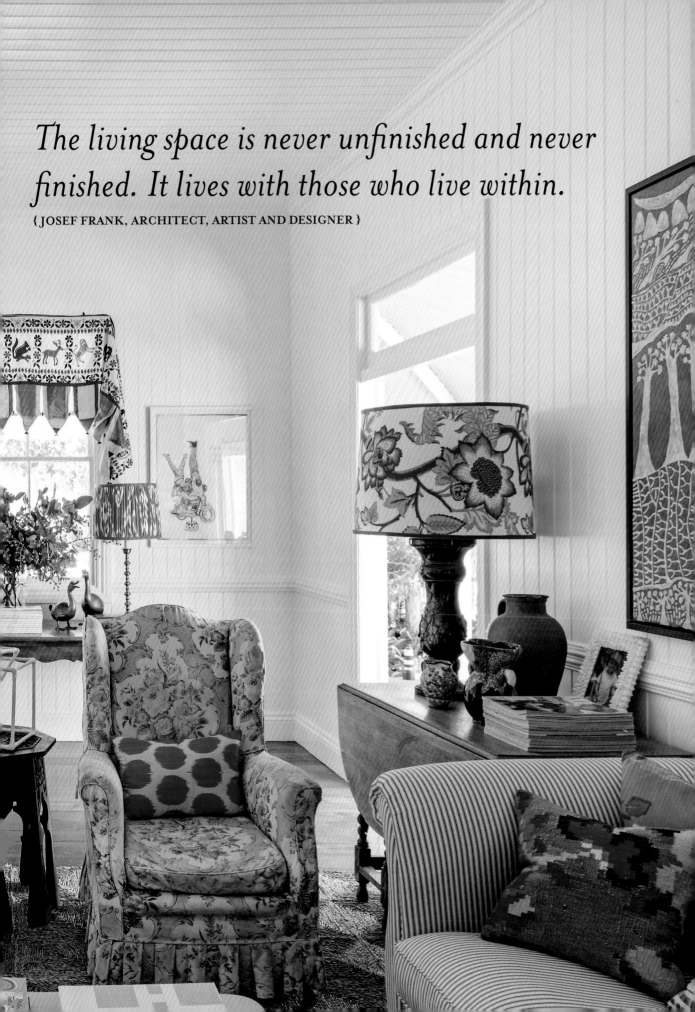

The living space is never unfinished and never finished. It lives with those who live within.

{ JOSEF FRANK, ARCHITECT, ARTIST AND DESIGNER }

Creative upcycling

Old furniture often has the most beautiful 'bones' and is of higher quality than a lot of manufactured items found in chain stores. I see its potential beyond faded and dated upholstery. Recycle old pieces of furniture by re-covering them, restaining or repainting the legs and even changing some of the detailing. Deep buttoning can be added or removed, or fringing and piping inserted to create a subtle contrast and enhance interest. Before buying a new piece of furniture, consider updating an old piece. It is unique, has history and adds a splash of difference and soul to your home. Best of all, you are bringing life back into something which may have otherwise been disposed of.

Be daring. We recently upcycled a client's dining chairs which had been upholstered in plain white canvas. We painted the upholstery of each chair in different colourful patterns and stripes. Totally unique, totally outrageous but totally fabulous! It's heartbreaking to find that when clients are downsizing, nobody in their family wants their furniture or collections. You shouldn't want every little thing your parents or grandparents owned, but incorporating a few family heirloom pieces, either upcycled or kept as-is, and mixed in with your own treasured pieces, makes for a home full of meaning and style. Please don't let your mum, dad or grandparents throw or give away their treasured pieces. You'll be surprised by what a coat of paint or new fabric can do, and most of the time it is cheaper than buying a brand new piece that has no family history or meaning.

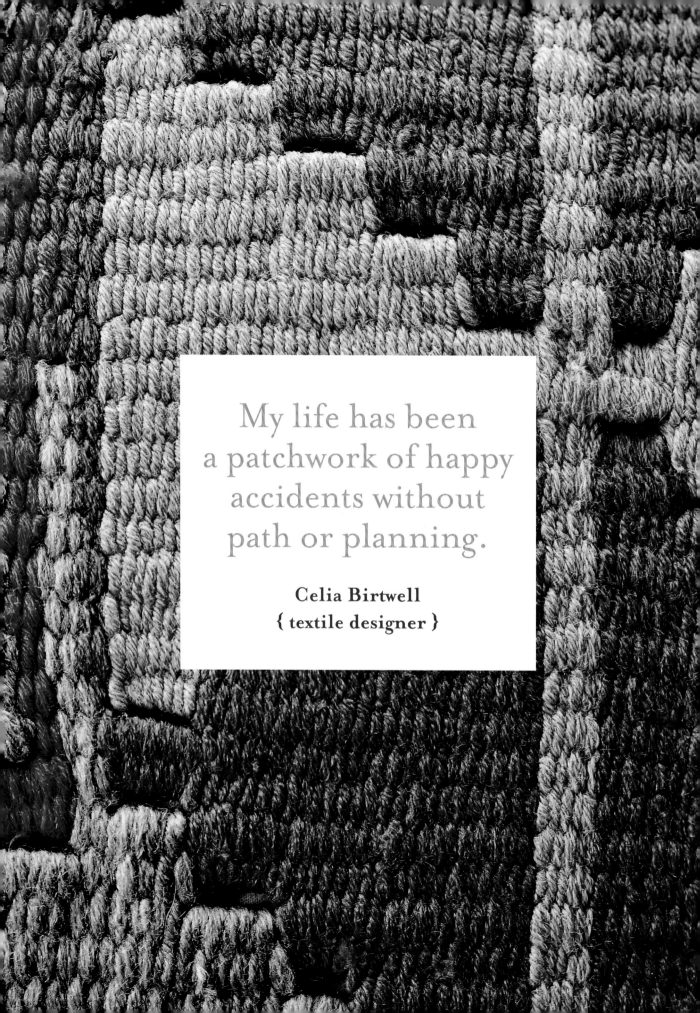

My life has been
a patchwork of happy
accidents without
path or planning.

Celia Birtwell
{ textile designer }

When embarking on a redecorating project,
be mindful of time lapses. Most people
underestimate how long a project can take.
When you are having things custom made, you
need to consider all the different elements which
go into their creation. For example, you may
be getting a new sofa made in a beautiful fabric
imported from Europe. The fabric can take
anywhere from two to four weeks to arrive, as long
as it is in stock and even longer if it isn't. It can
then take between six to fourteen weeks to have
the sofa made, depending on supplier lead-times,
workloads and so on. Sometimes in our fast paced
world we forget about all the different steps that
go into making something beautiful. We need to
be patient and not try to push and pressure people
along, as this will end up with a job not well done.
Just relax; as my mother always says, 'Good things
come to those who wait!'

with a happy face. "Doen[   ] coat, sir, if it's
you [   ]

"Thank you, Mr. Pegg[   ] giving him my
[   ]er coat to hang u[   ]
"So 'tis!" said [   ]otty [   ] my shoulders.
[   ]s a chip! Sit y[   ]t aint [   ]o use saying
[   ]rcome to you, but [   ]ine, kind and hearty."
"Thank you. M[   ]ure of that. Well,
[   ]ggotty!" [   ]g her a kiss. "And how are
[   ]ld w[   ]

[   ]a, h[   ] Mr. Peggotty, sitting down beside
[   ]d [   ] r[   ]hands in his sense of relief from
[   ]in the genuine heartiness of his
[   ]out a woman in the wureld, sir—as I
[   ]that [   ]to feel more easy in her mind than
de[   ]ooty by the departed, and the
[   ]d the departed done what was
[   ]whac was right by the departed;
[   ]"

[   ]ther!" said Mr. Peggotty.
[   ]t us, evidently sensible of
[   ]ces to recall the memory
[   ]wn! Cheer up, for your
[   ]ee if a good deal more

[   ]rned Mrs. Gummidge.
[   ]to be lone and lorn."

"Ye[   ]y, soothing her sorrows.
"I ain't a
person to[   ]s has had money left. Thinks
go too contrairy with me. I had better be a riddance."

"Why, how should I ever spend it without you?" said
Mr. Peggotty, with an air of serious remonstrance.
"What are you a talking on? Don't I want you more
now, than ever I did?"

"I know'd I was never wanted before!" cried Mrs.
Gummidge, with a pitiable whimper, "and now I'm told
so! How could I expect to be wanted, being so lone
and lorn, and so contrairy!"

Mr. Peggotty seemed very much shocked at himself for
having made a speech capable of this unfeeling construc-
tion, but was prevented from replying, by Peggotty's
pulling his sleeve, and shaking her head. After looking
T.C.

Establishing and working within your budget

In all reality, everyone has a budget and working within your budget is one of the most important aspects of decorating your home. Always try to consider what is going to give you the biggest bang for your dollar. I recently helped a client on a very tight budget inject some much-needed colour and atmosphere into her home. She needed some cushions, coffee table, lamp, sidetable and two new armchairs. She already had a tan leather sofa, a colourful painting, a patchwork crochet throw blanket and a black and natural striped floor rug she bought before asking me to help her. The floor rug was an unnecessarily expensive purchase and did nothing for the room. A cost-effective sisal matting rug would have been a much better investment. The remainder could have been used for some divine custom-made bright and colourful cushions, a beautiful lamp with an interesting patterned shade, and two colourful bespoke upholstered armchairs. These pieces would result in an immediate injection of colour and excitement as well as being pieces she could keep for a very long time! It is so important to spend money on pieces that will actually make a difference and improve the look, feel and comfort of your home, rather than buying a few expensive things that consume your budget and don't do much to enhance the overall environment.

*It is important to
really know what
colours you love and
those you dislike;
it's something I always
ask my clients at the
first meeting.*

Colour

Even though I'm an ambassador for clashing colour because it's so interesting, layered and beautiful, there are some colours I don't use in my home because I don't like them. The one colour I particularly dislike is maroon. Maybe because it was the colour of my school uniform. You will never see maroon in my home and if you do, that may be the day to throw in the towel!!

While I wholeheartedly embrace variety in colour combinations, there are some staples I always come back to, such as blue and white mixed with pink, yellow, orange and green. Pink continues to pop up in my work and yet it is the colour I am most often asked by clients not to use. It's funny, though, because they almost all end up with a little bit of pink. Pink is like a little ray of sunshine. It bursts through the other colours and brings unquestionable happiness to any room. As US fashion editor Diana Vreeland once said, 'I adore pink. It's the navy blue of India.'

Talking of blue, it forms a fantastic foundation upon which to layer other colours. It looks great with pink, orange, red, taupe, yellow and green. In its simplest form, it shines when mixed with pure, ethereal white. Blue and white is a classic colour combination almost everyone loves. I have created many rooms around this palette and come back to them with as much love as the day I installed them.

	Permanent Orange		Raw Umber
	Spectrum Yellow		Burnt Umber
	Ultramarine Violet		Indigo
	Indian Yellow		Light Red
	Yellow Ochre		Viridian
	Tasman Blue		Serpée
	P. Red Gold		Scarlet Lake
	Sap green		Windsor Blue
	Permanent rose		French Ultramarine
	Chinese white		Naples Yellow
	Brown Madder		Raw Sienna
	Cerulean Blue		Burnt Sienna
	Alyarin Crimson		Prussian
	Manganese Blue		Cobalt
	Rose Madder Genuine		Paynes Grey
			Windsor Violet

*I immediately recognise
a colour I love. It's really
an instant feeling for me.
Colour evokes immediate
emotional reaction,
as well as creates joy.*

{ *Thakoon Panichgul, fashion designer* }

When selecting a colour palette for clients, I usually start with either black or navy as the base colour. Choosing a dark colour provides a scheme with strength upon which a multitude of bright colours in patterns on fabrics, artwork and rugs can be layered. A colour I have never really been a huge lover of is brown. In the past I would never use it in a room. The funny thing is lately, though, I have become secretly very intrigued by brown. Maybe it's because I have been working in a divine house owned by a family who love a natural colour palette made up of lots of earthy browns, oranges and taupes. Being around this colour and using it in their home has led me to look at it in a whole new light. I believe no room, even the most colourful, should be without a bit of brown. Whether it's in the timber of a sidetable or sideboard, brown provides a grounding. It seems that I am constantly learning and trying new things based on experiences I have had. I'm contemplating a brown room myself, which even I find surprising! Nothing's set in stone, which is part of the joy of what I do.

When using bright colour, it is very important to mix it with textiles such as linen, hessian or sisal in natural colours. There really is a fine line; if you use too much colour with too few natural elements, the result will be an unattractive, fairy floss mess! It really is like making a cake — too much or too little of one ingredient can spoil the whole thing. The incorporation of natural colours and textures provides a much-needed grounding to the multitude of colours I tend to use.

BRIGHT COLOUR
+ NATURAL COLOUR
= COLOURFUL SUCCESS

Pattern

Pattern mixing is a large part of what I do. I make sure each client has a different combination of fabrics to keep their look unique, mixing florals, stripes, geometrics and abstract patterns to create a clashing and interesting collection. To get the right look, mix different pattern scales. Mix small patterns, medium patterns and large patterns together for enhanced interest. If you tire of pattern quickly, use it in the smaller, accessory pieces of your room, such as the scatter cushions, lampshades, small stools or chairs.

For me, no home should be without pattern.

*I always start
my scheme with
something I call
the trophy fabric.*

The trophy fabric

When selecting fabrics for a room, I always start with something I call the 'trophy fabric'. It is usually patterned, will have lots of colours and, despite its bravado, might only be used for a cushion, or on a small stool. Its colours will make the room more flexible by providing a diverse colour palette that can be referenced in the rest of the scheme. If, for instance, I'm using navy as my base colour, the multicoloured trophy fabric will feature navy somewhere in it.

Selecting a trophy fabric can be tricky as there are limited multicoloured fabrics (a fabric with four to six colours within the one design) out there. They're rare as they tend to be expensive to produce because of the number of different screens required to create them. But they're like little treasures. Safi Suzani by Kathryn Ireland is one that springs to mind. The multitude of colours and intricate pattern provide a perfect place to start many a scheme. Mexican mantel is also great for this as it is multicoloured and textured. Vintage or embroidered Indian textiles are great for filling this multicoloured void as well.

By using a range of multicoloured and multi-patterned fabrics on the pieces of furniture throughout your home, they will be able to adapt to all sorts of situations. Because you aren't going for a perfectly matching scheme for each room, this will allow you to move pieces around the house without disturbing the overall look. For example, you may decide to have an old ottoman which you have always used as a coffee table in your lounge room re-covered in a new fabric so it can then be placed as a bed-end stool in your bedroom. Select a fabric that works both in your bedroom and lounge room to give you the greatest flexibility.

Starting with the trophy fabric as inspiration for the whole room will dictate the other major choices for furniture and accessories. It's important to use a variety of types and scales of patterns. Aim to have at least: two florals ❧ a stripe ❧ a plain ❧ a check ❧ a geometric ❧ a small 'dobby' (spot, floral, pattern) ❧ an embroidered textile.

SOME OF MY FAVOURITE TROPHY FABRICS

Kathryn Ireland Safi Suzani ❧ *Schumacher Sunara Ikat* ❧ *Manuel Canovas Serendip* ❧ *Designers Guild Alexandria Lapis* ❧ *Robert Allen Wetherburns* ❧ *Robert Allen Kingsmill* ❧ *Thibaut Fishbowl* ❧ *Mexican otomi* ❧ *Quadrille Jacaranda*

FAVOURITE FABRICS

It's very hard to narrow down the huge array of amazing fabrics out there to a small list of favourites. My list of favourite fabrics is ever-evolving as new collections are released. In saying that, though, there seem to be a few I always come back to and have always loved. Quite often, it seems, these come from a small selection of established fabric houses that produce exceptional fabrics both in colour and quality.

SOME OF MY ALL-TIME FAVOURITE FABRIC HOUSES

Pierre Frey ❧ *Quadrille* ❧ *China Seas* ❧ *Manuel Canovas* ❧ *Raoul Textiles* *Kathryn Ireland* ❧ *Brunschwig & Fils* ❧ *Walter G* ❧ *GP & J Baker* *Etamine Thibaut* ❧ *Designers Guild*

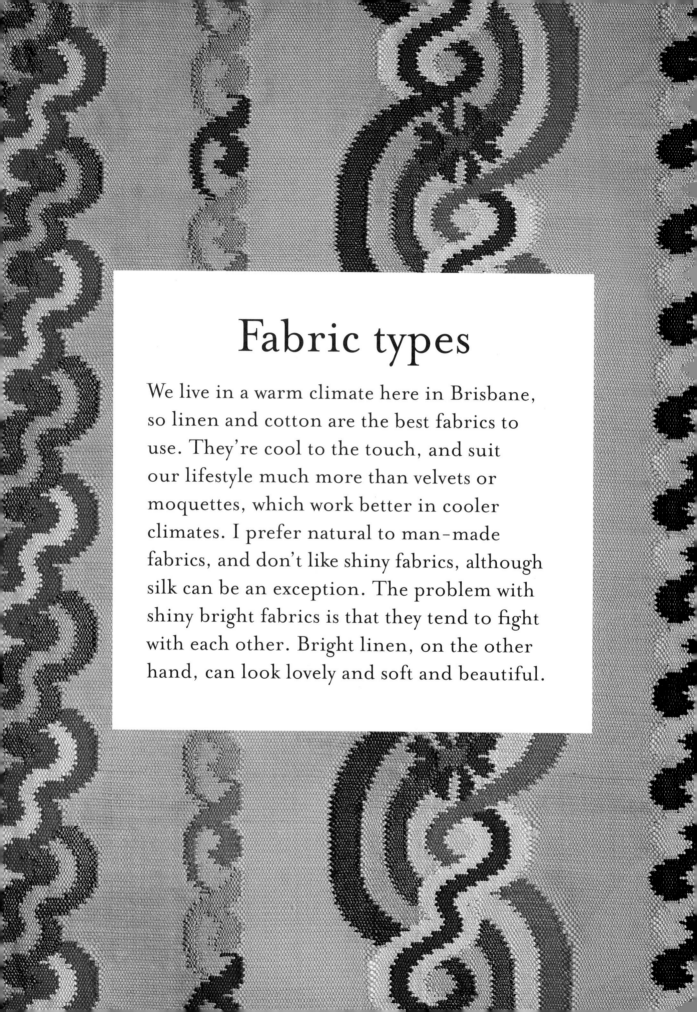

Fabric types

We live in a warm climate here in Brisbane, so linen and cotton are the best fabrics to use. They're cool to the touch, and suit our lifestyle much more than velvets or moquettes, which work better in cooler climates. I prefer natural to man-made fabrics, and don't like shiny fabrics, although silk can be an exception. The problem with shiny bright fabrics is that they tend to fight with each other. Bright linen, on the other hand, can look lovely and soft and beautiful.

- TICKING -

It's a fabric staple, and great on armchairs and sofas. A well-priced fabric, it lasts and lasts. My mother has had cane chairs on her verandah at the beach covered in blue and white ticking for about eight years, and it just keeps going and going, almost like an Eveready battery. Ticking is also a lovely background fabric. You can layer lots of fabulous pattern and colour on top of it in the form of cushions or throws, or you can pare it back to its simple self.

- LINEN -

This is fantastic for curtains, upholstery and lampshades. Its natural characteristics bring a grounding effect to the multicolouring on other pieces in a room. Patterned, printed linens are particularly lovely. Old fabric houses such as GP & J Baker produce some of the most beautiful patterned linen fabrics; florals with birds and fabulous colour combinations. The printed linens produced by Quadrille, China Seas and Alan Campbell are also wonderful. For durability when selecting an upholstery fabric, usually a cotton/linen mix is recommended over 100 percent linen.

If you are having a sofa or armchair upholstered or slipcovered in a linen fabric, be aware that it will stretch and become quite slouchy over time. We usually suggest backing linen prior to upholstering, as this will extend the life of your upholstery and the slouch factor won't become as much of a problem. In saying that, some people, including myself, love a bit of slouch!

- COTTON FLORALS, -
STRIPES & CHECKS

These fabrics look wonderful made into curtains, lampshades and cushions or even small, upholstered pieces. There's a crispness and informality to cotton. It's cool and lovely to use here in our hot Queensland climate, and looks fresh anywhere. Manuel Canovas and Brunschwig & Fils, both French fabric houses, produce some of the best cotton patterned florals and stripes.

- SILK -

Silk is suited to cooler climates, where the sun is not likely to make it disintegrate. If you're determined to use it, even if the climate's against it, back it for added protection or use a taffeta (polyester silk look) for longevity.

- VINTAGE TEXTILES -

A desirably unexpected vibe can be achieved when you throw a vintage textile into the mix. Whether you opt for a vintage Liberty or Sanderson floral or some fabulous antique ethnic textiles, such as Mexican otomi, Indonesian batik, Hmong embroidery or Turkish kilim, the look is all about being unique and offbeat, and very individual.

- OUTDOOR FABRICS -

For high traffic areas, both indoors and out, nothing beats outdoor fabrics. Use them on interior sofas in a sunny position – they won't fade like normal interior fabrics. They are a great choice, too, for children's areas and wet areas as they are also mould-resistant.

- VELVET -

Being cosy, warm and soft, this is another one for the cooler climates. But even in warmer parts of the world, it can look lovely in small doses, on the backs of beautifully detailed ethnic cushions or on a small stool that isn't used all the time.

Cushions

One of the most exciting and effective elements of any scheme can be the array of cushions custom made for sofas, armchairs and beds. The small elements make the most impact, and cushions are one of those very important small elements that can either make or break a room. Almost like wearing a fabulous multicoloured jewelled necklace with a plain black dress — it's all about the necklace — and it's exactly the same with cushions. Husbands have a hard time being convinced of this, as it is a known fact that most men think cushions are a complete waste of money. However, as we all know, and thankfully for me, the woman usually wins and the cushions are made and delivered and instantly finish the space perfectly. The cushions I design for clients are made in the most exquisite fabrics which are either imported, hand embroidered or constructed out of vintage materials, and trimmed with fabulous braid or ruche.

The special textiles and workmanship which goes into every cushion we make often results in a higher price than a ready-made substitute. The handmade bespoke version will still be around when its cheaper counterpart has been turned into a laundry rag! One customer came to me years after I did her house to tell me that while her unique set of cushions still sits proudly on her sofa, loved and cherished, most of her friends have since been through three or four rounds of inexpensive, ready-made cushions.

If you can't buy your own collection of special cushions upfront, start with a couple and then add to them over time. This way, you will end up with the most gorgeous collection that you'll adore for years to come. Adding new cushions will be like a breath of fresh air for even the plainest or most outdated sofa. If a quick fix is needed to give your room a lift, head to your local decorator and put together a beautiful collection of fabrics and have some divine cushions made. They will change your life!!

The other wonderful thing about cushions is that they can be changed around so easily, creating a whole new look. The more mismatched your collection, the easier it is to pull cushions in and out and move them around. Have two sets of cushions for your lounge room if you can; one set for winter and the other for summer. This keeps things interesting and, as the saying goes, 'A change is as good as a holiday'.

Another important, but often overlooked, element of great cushions is the inserts. Choosing pure feather, or feather and foam inserts and overstuffing your cushions will keep them looking fat and sitting well for years, whereas cheap synthetic alternatives will look deflated and tired very quickly. When having cushions made, insist on having an invisible zip so you can't see any seams, zips or joins when the cushion is placed on your sofa, armchair or bed.

Have at least five cushions on a two-seater or two-and-a-half-seater sofa and seven to nine cushions for a three-seater or four-seater sofa. Always odd, never even. That breaks up the perfectness of it, which is generally a good rule. Life's not perfect, so why have a perfect house? Oh, and mix up the shapes and sizes too — some larger, some smaller, some rectangular. The best results come from a collection that isn't thought about too seriously and intensely, yet one that is put together with serious clash and imperfection.

There are many ways you can select a mismatched collection of cushions. Usually the use of two 50 cm square cushions, two 45 cm square cushions and one 40 cm by 30 cm rectangular cushion on a sofa is a good arrangement of size and proportion. You can have each one made in a completely different fabric or, if you want a little bit of repetition which is sometimes a good thing, have the two larger cushions made in the same fabric and then all the other ones made in different fabrics. For flexibility, it can also be exciting to have cushions made using one fabric on the front and an alternative fabric on the back — this way you can turn them around for a fresh look. If you want to pick out a particular colour in the fabric, add piping in a plain colour. This brings strength and detail to the mismatch.

An important secret
is that cushions should never
be placed on their point. I was
taught this a very long time ago,
and told it was the telltale sign
of an uneducated decorator.
Cushions must always be placed
on the square.

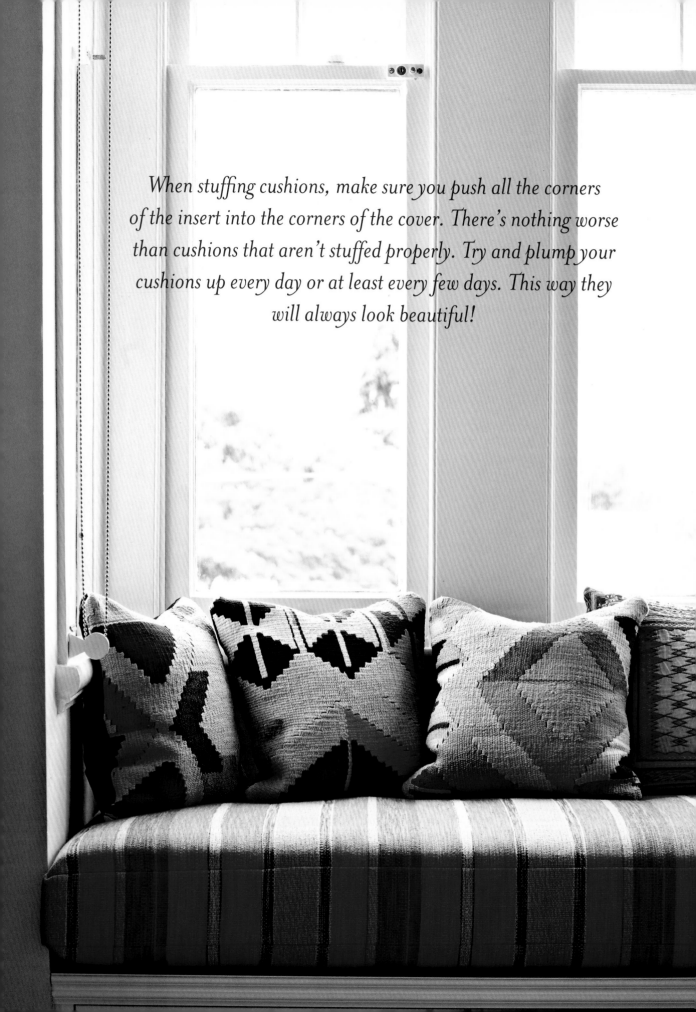

When stuffing cushions, make sure you push all the corners
of the insert into the corners of the cover. There's nothing worse
than cushions that aren't stuffed properly. Try and plump your
cushions up every day or at least every few days. This way they
will always look beautiful!

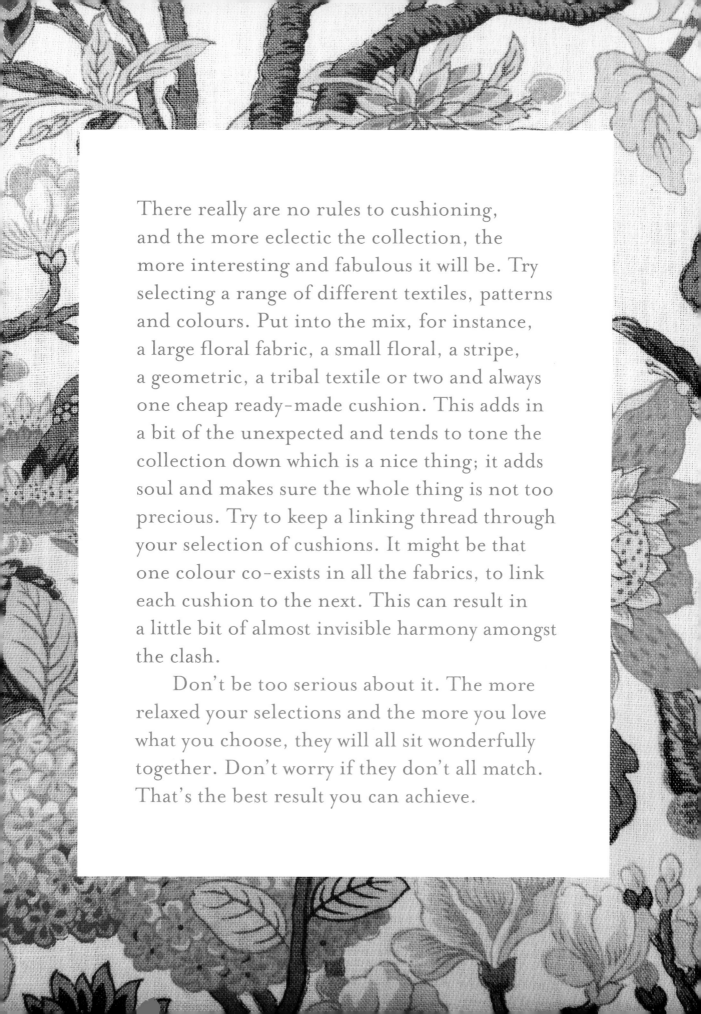

There really are no rules to cushioning, and the more eclectic the collection, the more interesting and fabulous it will be. Try selecting a range of different textiles, patterns and colours. Put into the mix, for instance, a large floral fabric, a small floral, a stripe, a geometric, a tribal textile or two and always one cheap ready-made cushion. This adds in a bit of the unexpected and tends to tone the collection down which is a nice thing; it adds soul and makes sure the whole thing is not too precious. Try to keep a linking thread through your selection of cushions. It might be that one colour co-exists in all the fabrics, to link each cushion to the next. This can result in a little bit of almost invisible harmony amongst the clash.

Don't be too serious about it. The more relaxed your selections and the more you love what you choose, they will all sit wonderfully together. Don't worry if they don't all match. That's the best result you can achieve.

Mix up cushion detailing.
Make some with piped
edges, some with plain or
topstitched edges and some
trimmed with a ruche or
cord. This also adds to the
mismatch and imperfection
of the collection.

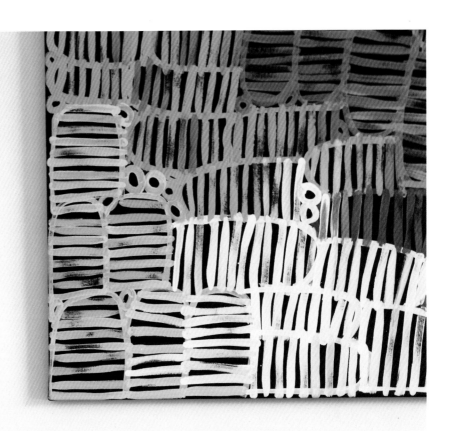

*While I may have
become renowned for
my love of colour and
abandoned approach
to using it, I like it
to be grounded on
a canvas of beautifully
simple white.*

The perfect backdrop

White (the right white) provides the perfect backdrop for your furniture and collections. Upon its crisp foundations, you can layer your fabulous bits and pieces, books, artwork, rugs, collections, fabrics and furniture. One of the good things about using white as a background on surfaces such as walls, floors, cabinetry and even sofas, armchairs and bedding is that you can layer lots of colour on top or strip it back to its bare self and simplify. It's just so flexible.

White is not just the perfect choice for interiors either. I have a thing for white houses. Our first house was white, our second house was white, our beach cottage is white and our current house, the house I hope we will stay in forever, is also white. When clients ask me what colour they should paint their house, I always tell them white. The fact is that white houses never date. They look especially lovely when they are surrounded by lots of gardens or big green luscious trees and lots of green neatly trimmed grass. There is nothing prettier. Oh, maybe a pink house could be prettier!

Don't be fooled; not all whites are right. Some of the best ones are Wattyl Magic White, Dulux Vivid White and Porter's Paints Absolute White. If in doubt, hold your paint swatch against a sheet of white paper. If they are comparable in colour and crispness, then that white is right!

A lot of people like to use off-white; I'm not a fan because it dilutes the clarity of colours and patterns placed against it. The warmth that some might argue can be brought through an off-white can easily be introduced in other ways, such as the inclusion of antique furniture, timber floors and the patina of well-loved heirlooms.

If you want an all-white look, paint every trim and ceiling and wall in the same white. Don't paint the walls one white and the ceilings and trims a different one; it can become too complicated and busy. Tradespeople such as painters and tilers will try to advise you to mix the whites, but stick to your guns and don't be dissuaded. You will end up with the result you had always hoped to achieve.

If you want an all-white look,
paint every trim and ceiling and wall
in your house in the same white.

Wallpaper

Wallpaper can be a scary choice for many people, who may view it as a more permanent option than paint. I am particularly fond of using wallpaper in small rooms or awkward spaces. It's great in entry foyers, hallways, powder rooms, pantries, walk-in wardrobes and installed into the backs of cupboards and bookcases and shelving. If you are a person who tires of pattern quickly, you will most likely enjoy it for longer if you install the wallpaper in these smaller, less visited areas of your home.

There are many papers to choose from these days, and making a decision can be overwhelming. To help in that regard, first decide on a colour palette and then decide on a pattern. As it's such a dominant feature, wallpaper is one of the first things you should choose in a room. On top of this, paper the entire room rather than a feature wall. It looks much better if the background of a space is consistent; a single wall of wallpaper ends up looking disjointed, especially where the pattern finishes at a corner and the paint colour starts.

Does big patterned wallpaper in a small space make it look even smaller? Maybe it does, but does that really matter? Do you love the pattern? Do you love the colour? Then just run with it. It will look striking and fabulous and confident.

Wallpapered walls can look totally breathtaking when layered with paintings. By layering your artwork or family photos on top of a wallpapered wall, you are adding your very own touch and personality. It astonishes me the number of people over the years who have sighed with admiration as they walk into our wallpapered hallway at Black & Spiro which is layered with a big collection of old pictures and photos and mirrors and plates. Hopefully it has inspired some people to do something similar within their own homes, which can create so much interest and lots of wonderful comments from visitors too!

Wallpaper isn't something I've always been fond of. I'd liked the idea of plain white walls, but then Porter's Paints asked me to design a range. I had been pushing for them to do fabric, but they were keen to do wallpaper. My designs for them have grown out of my love of textiles and my love of art — I wanted to have the hand-drawn look in all of them. I love the whole process of designing wallpaper, coming up with ideas, working through the concept boards, working with an illustrator. And in the process, I've come to appreciate wallpaper and now use it a lot more than I would have imagined.

Art cluster walls

If you know anything at all about me, you know that
I love paintings and photographs hung in clusters on walls.
It could be family photographs; the mix of photos
with paintings creates an exciting visual effect.
When hanging an art/photo wall, as usual there are no rules.
Sometimes people choose to frame all the photos in the
same style and coloured frame, or they might choose a single
colour and mix up the style of the actual frame. A great way
of doing it is to mix framed and unframed pieces — it results
in an interesting and layered grouping. Whatever your
choice, make sure you do it with impact; lots of pieces are
best, and they can even be hung all the way to the floor or
just propped up against a wall. I prefer to use a mix of frames
and suggest not to worry too much about dated frames as
once they are in the mix, you don't even notice them.

An art cluster wall changed the feeling of my mum's
bedroom (*right*), making it feel so cosy and lived-in. She said
it made all her old things new again; we included pieces of
my great-grandmother's, my grandmother's paintings, and
ones painted by her best friend and drawn by my brothers.

I dream
my painting
and then
I paint
my dream

Van Gogh

five, six, pick
up sticks.

- HOW TO HANG ARTWORK -

*

The trick to hanging cluster walls is to first lie the paintings
and photographs down on the floor in a layout you like.

*

When I hang a wall, I try to make sure no painting or photo
or mirror lines up. Break all the lines to create a haphazard effect.

*

Use an array of different sized pieces. A mix of small,
medium and large pieces creates a more interesting end result.

*

After deciding on a layout design that works, take a photo
you can refer back to while doing the hanging.

*

If you're not handy, have a professional picture hanger
hang the wall. This saves on unnecessary holes, wonky
pictures, uneven spacing and tears of frustration.

*

When selecting the pieces for your art cluster wall, consider
using a mix of children's artwork, vintage paintings, modern
abstract paintings, mirrors, framed mementoes, family photographs,
even baskets or old plates or taxidermy.

*

Nothing looks better than a child's painting hanging
next to a collectable piece of art. To keep the various pieces
on your wall straight, once they are all hung, pop a little piece
of Blu-Tack in the bottom corners of each piece.

Collections

If a stranger came into my home, they would probably see lots of meaningless things. But I see special pieces which hold memories from places I have been, people I love and experiences I have had. Any vignette in my home features treasures I cherish; every piece must hold a special memory or be of personal value and significance. These treasures can be easily moved or stored, and it's exciting to rediscover special things you haven't seen in a while, and handle them and reminisce and consider where next to display them. Instead of throwing out or giving away things you might be tired of, pack them up and store them so you don't miss out on the joy they can give you all over again in a few years' time.

It's so interesting to see what other people surround themselves with; I am constantly intrigued by the collections they have in their homes. Home to me is the most important and special place on earth, where I find solace, rest and happiness, and where I surround myself with only the things I love. It's not about having the latest and greatest; it's about filling your home with things you absolutely adore, cherish and hold close to your heart. Photographer Oberto Gili once quoted a landscape architect friend of his to explain how decor reflects the inhabitant: 'Unless a home becomes a love affair, it is not a success.' He continued, 'You have to love every single little thing — if it doesn't have a memory, a story, it doesn't count.'

Collections of things on display within a house add the owner's personality to what is otherwise a blank canvas. Don't be afraid to pull out your grandmother's old china or your mother's cherished vase as it is special and should be used and not hidden away forever. Why have beautiful things if they are stored away, not to be seen and enjoyed?

If you don't have a collection, think about what you love and what you would like to collect one day. Some things you might consider are old plates, shells, vases, Depression glass, silverware, Christmas ornaments, botanical prints, maps, blue and white china or antique textiles. I have started to collect old blue and white dinner plates in varying patterns and designs, and old, mismatched silver cutlery to add variety when setting the table for special dinners.

Starting a collection is fantastic for family and friends as it makes it much easier for them at Christmas and birthdays. It's lovely for you, too, as you will receive gifts you love rather than things that might go into the back of a cupboard! My sister-in-law Pip recently started collecting old copperware. Her collection is growing quite rapidly as family and friends give her special pieces. It will be lovely for her in time to look back and remember who gave her which piece and for what particular occasion in her life.

As well as blue and white china, my collections include decorative boxes, silverware, shells, antique jugs, textiles, old timber millinery hat blocks, old garden pots, table linens and books, just to name a few. I don't tend to display them all together in a glass cabinet but, instead, they are placed on tables and shelving, mixed up with other bits and pieces I have collected over time. I have also inherited my mother's love of collecting beach hats. In a similar way to using baskets as decoration, stacks of hats can also be a great look in a beach house. Stack them on old hat blocks on tables and sideboards. By incorporating usable, everyday things like hats and baskets into the decoration of our homes, whether they are at the beach, in the country or in the city, we are able to achieve a very personal, simple, cost-effective yet stylish look.

A mismatched group of blue and white ginger jars placed in an armoire with glass doors or a few placed into a vignette on a table or sideboard look so beautiful. They also look wonderful filled with peonies, lilies, frangipani branches and even Australian native flowers. My mother has been collecting ginger jars for as long as I can remember and I seem to have caught her blue and white ginger jar bug. When selecting them, look for ones of varying size and pattern; this way your collection will be unique and more interesting.

Collecting and decorating over time

When Brad and I got married and were setting up our first home, I admit to making a few rash decisions when it came to buying furniture. It was because I wanted to have a beautiful house as quickly as possible. The nesting instincts kicked in at a million miles an hour and, while I'm glad I started to collect antique furniture from such a young age, I do look back now and wonder why I was in such a hurry. For instance, some people were coming to dinner, so I rushed out and bought a cabinet I didn't love, just because I wanted the house to look nice! That seems so stupid now. It's much better to find the perfect piece instead of a second-best alternative just to fill a space. The hunt for that elusive perfect piece becomes part of it – it's fine to wait, and better to have nothing than to fill a space with something you don't truly love.

Collecting over time also enables you to see where you really need particular items and what prerequisites are important for the function each will serve. Having said all that, though, architect Bill Ingram's philosophy for collecting the perfect pieces over time is encapsulated in the following quote: 'When you see something perfect, buy it. If you don't have a place for it, you're going to have to force yourself. But eventually you'll wind up with a house full of things you love.'

Antiques transcend fashion and trends. Not only do they guarantee a unique look and not a space reminiscent of a catalogue shoot, you will also have lovely memories associated with the time, place and people you were experiencing when you bought each piece.

Homes should be ever-evolving reflections of our ever-evolving selves and, in adding bits and pieces to our homes along the way, we are refreshing them in small, uplifting doses. A stagnant, predictable space will not only become dull and dreary very quickly, it will also be a space that requires a major overhaul in five years' time.

MARY MCDONALD INTERIORS

THE KELLY WEARSTLER

大明宣德年製

The art of arranging

Some may wonder why I seem to have an obsession with lovely things placed on tables and chests and mantels. It must stem back to my younger years watching my mother arranging flowers, shells, paintings, books and bits on tables around our house. I remember wondering what on earth she was doing, and what the point of it all was – even thinking she was very strange – but it seems that now I, too, love moving things around on tables and mantels within my home and my store. I obviously observed my mother's wonderful ability to arrange things and subconsciously absorbed the art of it in my early years. There is something so therapeutic about arranging objects and collections, and flowers in vases. It's wonderful playing and experimenting with different pieces to create interesting and unexpected tablescapes and vignettes.

Nothing looks better than a table against a wall or behind a sofa that has so much stuff on it you can barely see the top of it. Having said that, a little table space is a good thing as it allows the objects to 'breathe' and be seen and appreciated. Creating vignettes and clusters on tables, shelves and mantels within your home shows personality and a love of beautiful things.

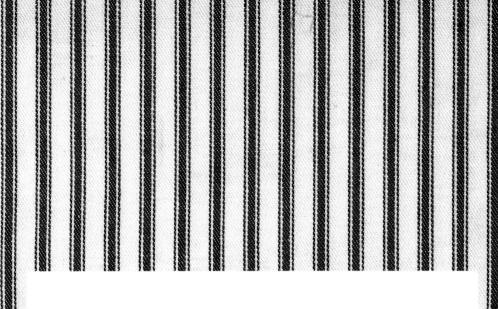

- TIPS ON ARRANGING -

Aim for tablescapes or vignettes filled with quirky objects
of varying heights.

❧

Use stacks of books or magazines to elevate objects.

❧

Placing items in a zigzag arrangement is always
pleasing to the eye.

❧

Odd numbers are better than even when arranging pieces.

❧

The very best vignettes are filled with imperfection
and the unexpected, therefore drawing you in for a closer
inspection of the special things that co-exist.

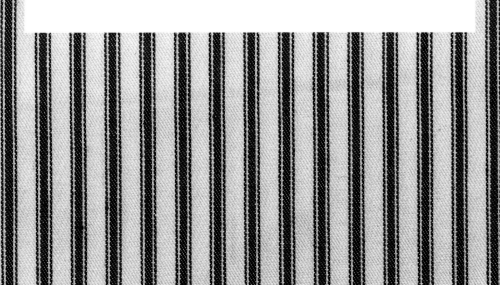

JOHN OLSEN JOURNEYS INTO THE 'YOU BEAUT C

To create visual impact, grouping like items together in cabinets or shelves can not only be of organisational value but can also be striking and beautiful.

- SUGGESTIONS FOR TABLESCAPES -
AND VIGNETTES

Large trays stacked with magazines or books.

❦

A clam shell which can be filled with fruit such as lemons,
oranges or limes for added colour. Bowls of shells or pine cones.

❦

Photos in beautiful antique silver frames. Special items
found on holidays or overseas trips.

❦

Large arrangements of local flora, such as banksia. Found natural
objects such as banksia husks or pandanus nuts.

❦

Old timber or decorative boxes, which are also great
for storing the TV remote controls.

❦

Ginger jars. Old collected copperware or silverware.
Potted succulents or cacti.

❦

Hat blocks, sculpture or children's pottery.

❦

Candle jars, hurricane lamps or lanterns.

❦

A large collection of blue and white plates hung
together on a wall in your kitchen.

There are no rules; anything you love can be used to fill a tablescape or vignette.

Surprising uses of furniture

When selecting furniture, consider alternative uses for pieces. Creativity in the use of items allows pieces to be interchangeable and flexible. In kitchens, use old pieces of furniture in place of cabinetry. It gives the space a more lived-in, individual look and, if planned properly, you can incorporate new cabinetry and old furniture pieces together in a kitchen to create a very workable and attractive space.

In my own kitchen I have an antique chest of drawers, which houses my napery collection, and an old French armoire put to use as our pantry. I love the mix-up ratio of furniture to cabinetry and feel as though my kitchen belongs to me and shows my love of thinking outside the square.

I always keep an eye out for old butcher's blocks. Whenever I've had them in the shop, they've sold within days. They went to new homes to be used as sidetables, placed bedside or between sofas with a lamp placed on top. This is a perfect example of creative upcycling of a piece of furniture that in this day and age has now been replaced with a modern-day alternative.

A great storage idea is to cover an old table with a piece of fabric, reaching right down to the floor on all sides. You can hide the DVD player and any number of other things under there, and nobody would have a clue!

Don't be set in your ways when looking for possible furniture options. For example, you may fall in love with an antique chest of drawers, so why not consider putting it on one side of your bed as a bedside table and then placing a smaller piece on the other side? You don't have to have perfect, matching bedside tables. Or use a chair as a bedside table. With this solution, it creates a less contrived, interesting look in your bedroom and you get to buy the pieces you love which you initially didn't think you would be able to fit anywhere. Think outside of the box and consider different uses for pieces of furniture you stumble across and fall in love with.

part 03

....

{ ROOMS }

Now that we've talked about how to achieve
the look you're after, let's work out exactly
what furniture you need in each room,
and think about what decisions you need
to make along the way.

{ THE LOUNGE ROOM }

Several pieces of furniture are fundamental to every home. These are the items that require careful consideration before making the leap to purchase. Comfortable seating is essential to make your house inviting and relaxing, both to you and your guests. Everyone has their own likes and dislikes when it comes to comfort – taller people prefer deep sofas and shorter people tend to like the opposite. So finding the right balance is important. A sofa is one of the key investment pieces you want to be able to hold onto and not have to replace every half-decade. The sofa acts as the room's anchor, whereas accessories can be changed over time. Remember, comfort is paramount!

- CHOOSING A SOFA -

Choose one with a small or mid-profile arm, never a large arm as this style dates quickly and can take up too much space. A classic shape with small profile arms works better than of-the-moment styles.

Check with the manufacturer to make sure it has a hardwood timber frame. Hardwood is nice and sturdy, which is what you need for a sofa.

Opt for a feather and foam wrap seat cushion. The foam core ensures long-term shape stability, while the feather and foam wrap affords that lovely 'sinking in' comfort we long for at the end of the day, therefore ticking two prerequisites, comfort and practicality.

In terms of selecting a fabric, always lean towards a plain fabric as its simplicity increases longevity and flexibility. By going plain on your sofa, you can use a wonderful mix of patterns and colours in the scatter cushions you place on it. Further down the track, if you tire of some of the fabrics you have chosen, it's much more economical to change your cushions than to re-cover the entire sofa.

Another option is to opt for a slipcovered sofa, which is perfect for a relaxed homely look as well as being extremely practical and easy to get cleaned. In the past, I have made summer and winter sets of slipcovers for clients to allow for change as the seasons dictate. This will also prolong the life of the covers by limiting wear. Slipcovers are often produced by sofa manufacturers, or your local decorating store can organise to have these made for you.

Finally, if your existing sofa's comfortable and a good shape, get it re-covered. Buy well from the start and re-covering will be an option for many decades to come. Not only will it be more economical in the long run, but you'll be avoiding the modern-day offence of discarding a perfectly good item, only to replace it with something similar.

- ARMCHAIRS -

Avoid being run of the mill by opting for mismatched sofa and armchair combinations instead of purchasing a matching suite. Armchairs in a different style and covered in different fabric from the sofa allow for flexibility. Look for old chairs to re-cover; if there's room for two chairs in the lounge room, there's nothing better than to have them of different styles and upholstered in different fabrics. Armchairs are a great place to introduce some beautiful pattern; they look great covered in floral, striped and geometric designs.

    Old chairs have fabulous proportions and, often, divine turned timber legs that may be hidden by a skirt. Make sure you lift up their skirts as I'm sure you will find some seriously good legs underneath!! Get the chairs re-covered and remove the skirt to show off their legs.

    If you have a low-back sofa, go for armchairs with higher backs to add interest. This up-and-down effect adds to an overall exciting, unique and eclectic look. The other thing to consider is that these non-conforming chairs can then be used in other rooms when it comes time for an update down the track. The right chair can always be moved into a bedroom or guest room for a completely new look.

- THE ROUND SIDETABLE -

One of my favourite pieces of furniture is the extra large round sidetable, found in almost every lounge room I create. It is usually old, and may have originally been used as a kitchen dining table. The best ones measure anywhere between 70 cm and 110 cm in diameter, depending on the size of the room, and between 70 cm and 80 cm in height. Place them between two sofas in a lounge room, as the round shape breaks the line of the square or rectangular room and contrasts beautifully with the rectangular sofas. To provide contrasting heights, sit the round table higher than the arms of the sofas. Place a table lamp with a handmade shade on top as this adds additional height and ambient light. I'm always on the search for round tables or even hexagonal tables for this use and whenever I find one, I buy it!

- LAMPS & LAMPSHADES -

One of the most important, yet often overlooked, aspects of a good interior is lighting. Obviously it is vital in order to carry out basic tasks, but lighting sets the mood of the room. Whether it is overhead, wall, lamp or candlelight, your choice will have a huge impact on the way people feel in the space.

Opt for vintage lamp bases that can be used as-is, or repainted as required and topped with a handmade fabric lampshade. Old lamps can't be bought in chain stores, so straightaway you are guaranteed to have a piece that is special and unique. They they can be inexpensive, too – I found one of my favourite lamps at a flea market for $25.

Another idea is to turn an old vase or bottle into a table lamp. Over the years we have upcycled many unique pieces into lamps. I recently turned an old green porcelain plant stand into a divine lamp for our lounge room at home. No one else will have anything like it!

When scouring antique shops or markets for lamps, check to see if the electrics are appropriate for your needs; sometimes, if the item has been imported, it may need to be rewired to Australian standards and, while this is neither an expensive nor difficult task, it is something to be mindful of.

When selecting a lampshade for your lamp base, think about where the base is going to be placed and whether or not it needs a patterned shade to add interest to an area, or a plain shade if it is going into an already busy space. I love to use both small patterned fabrics and large-scale patterns on lampshades depending on the base and the room it is going into. If you can stretch your funds, a handmade shade rather than a bonded hard-back shade is, of course, the most desirable option.

Every room needs at least one lamp but the more the merrier, I say! Lamps are like cushions – you can't have a beautiful home without them. Don't dismiss the use of lamps in your home; they are one of the key ingredients to creating ambience and comfort. In my own home, it's most often only the lamps that are turned on at night, as I love their warm, cosy and welcoming glow.

- COFFEE TABLES -

A coffee table is the perfect stage for stacks of well-read books, vases of colourful flowers, collections of antique boxes and the like, but the presence of such items requires a table large enough to hold them. That table is often hard to come by – in fact, I've found it's often the most difficult to come by piece of furniture. Most standard sized coffee tables are too small for lavish displays, or too small for anything, really.

One way around this is to find a suitable sized dining table and cut the legs off. The old style kitchen table makes for a great coffee table too. My mum has had one at our family beach house for years which used to belong to my grandfather. She recognised its potential and snapped it up. These days it's stacked with Mum's favourite books and collections and, when we visit during summer, it's good for throwing our feet on while we're lounging on the sofa.

When cutting down an old table, consider a finished height somewhere between 40 cm and 45 cm.

- TELEVISIONS -

The 'T word', the one that men love and women loathe, is one that provides a challenge in creating homely, beautiful interiors. As much as it might offend our decorating sensibilities, the television is a modern-day essential and so we need to get creative. You can disguise the monstrosity within a large built-in bookcase, where it can fade into the business of surrounding books and objects. Alternatively, when placed on top of an antique chest of drawers, in the midst of an art cluster wall, the beauty surrounding it diverts attention away from the big black screen. If you want to hide the television completely, a large antique armoire will give it a suitably private home. Or, best of all, banish it to another room altogether.

- INTERCHANGEABLE PIECES -

There are some pieces of furniture with such an ability to multitask that they become invaluable. These are the pieces you can use as a lamp table, sidetable, bedside table, extra seating, a surface to display your collections, or even on a verandah with a big fern or orchid on top for decoration. An example of this is my obsession with gypsy tables, those tables made out of sticks, bamboo and/or cane and looking as if they have a tree trunk as their base. My brother bought me one for Christmas years ago, and I've always treasured it. If you see one of these quirky tables in your travels, make sure you pick it up and put it somewhere special — it will be one of those pieces you will love and keep forever.

- RUGS -

Rugs are the grounding element in a room, and look best when big enough for all furniture to fit on top. This creates the illusion of a large expanse in a poky room, while also allowing you to break up a very large open plan area into smaller, intimate parts as required. Custom-made sisal rugs are usually my preference as their natural characteristics establish a neutral yet textural foundation for the range of colours used elsewhere in the space. Some people don't like the rough feel of sisal; you can get a more cushioned effect by using a thick underlay.

Other suitable options are kilim rugs (great as hall runners) and old Persian rugs which, when placed in otherwise neutral spaces such as under a dining table or in a kitchen or hallway, provide an injection of colour. Use a small one as a bathmat in a crisp, all-white bathroom, but if you're using it in wet areas, make sure you give it a good airing as needed, and have it steam cleaned regularly to avoid a build-up of mildew and mould. It's important to find a good quality underlay to place under your rugs, as this will stop them slipping.

- CERAMIC DRUM STOOLS -

My mother has been using Asian blue and white ceramic drum stools
as sidetables for decades. They are flexible, and these days are a popular
piece of occasional furniture that can sit next to an armchair, ready
to put a drink or book on, or can be used as a stool, indoors or out.
I also love to place one beside my bath for my magazines, a candle
or a drink.

- OTTOMANS -

Upholstered ottomans, custom made in a size to suit, make wonderful
coffee tables in lounge rooms or, in particular, rooms with televisions.
Place a big rattan tray on top, piled with books and treasured objects.
The soft padding makes for a lovely comfortable place to throw your
legs when lying down to read a book or watch the TV. These pieces can
also be used when you have guests and need extra seating. To extend
the life of your ottoman coffee table, have it made as a slipcovered
piece so that it can be easily cleaned if an accident occurs.

{ THE DINING ROOM }

- THE DINING TABLE -

You should only buy a dining table once, or at the very most twice, in your lifetime. Brad and I bought our antique dining table from Brisbane antique dealer Nick Wallrock just before we were married, with some of our family members contributing to it for our wedding present. The French parquetry-top table is one of our most treasured pieces, which we will use for the rest of our lives.

An antique table will never date; to change the look, just change the chairs. When deciding on a table, consider how many people you have in your family and how many people you generally have for dinner. Another consideration is where the legs on the table are situated. A central pedestal, or legs situated at the very ends of the table are preferable, as inset legs can get in the way of dining chair placement, especially when extra place settings are required.

- DINING CHAIRS -

I love a harlequin — mismatched — set of dining chairs; a couple of antique French ladder backs, an upholstered Louis dining chair, a couple of bentwood ones, a few modern chairs. This look is so lovely and can even be a bit of fun with family members choosing their favourite chair to sit on each night at the family dinner!

Upholster each chair in a different fabric. If you're daring, you could cover your chairs in a plain white canvas and paint them in different patterns or colours. We recently did this on some antique French dining chairs — they're now a big talking point at the client's dinner parties. There's nothing like creating something so different it ends up being the topic of conversation at a party!!

It's important to choose comfortable chairs. It's odd that people don't think about that. It's nice to linger around the table; if the chairs are uncomfortable, nobody will want to sit on them.

Check that the chairs you are considering buying will fit comfortably under the table when you're sitting down. There's nothing worse than a chair so high there's no room for your legs under the table, or so low you need a cushion.

{ THE BEDROOM }

- BEDHEADS -

My bedroom is my place of solace, my favourite place in the entire
world. Find your own space within your home and make it special for
you. I'm definitely a fan of upholstered bedheads — they're soft and
luxurious to lean against while reading in bed. On top of that, they
provide an opportunity for using beautiful fabric. There are many
shapes to choose from, but a plain classic shape is the best option.
This look will stand the test of time, whereas a cutting-edge design is
more likely to date. Choose either a full-length bedhead, which goes
to the floor, or short panel, which finishes by the base. A full-length
panel attached to the wall behind the bed is preferable, as you don't
get any of that ugliness where the panel joins the base, which is the
case with the short panel. I recently had a new upholstered bedhead
made for our bedroom and, two nights after it was installed, our
two-year-old son, Max, decided to draw all over it with a green crayon.
An option to combat these occurrences is to have a slipcover made.
This allows for easy removal for cleaning when little accidents happen,
and you can also have different covers made for winter and summer.

- CUSTOM-MADE VALANCES -

Once you've had a custom-made, fitted valance made by my
workroom, you will never turn back! If I had to choose one very
special thing to have in my bedroom, that would be it. I can't tolerate
ready-made valances that move and fly around the bed every time
you make it. Our valances are made not only to your exact bed
measurements, but they have a wonderful fitted sheet underneath the
skirt that fits around the base and holds everything in place. You can
select a simple tailored style or a pretty gathered style, and the fabric
options are endless. This is one of those special items in your house
that, although expensive to have made, will last a lifetime.

- BEDSIDE TABLES -

Mismatched bedside tables in a bedroom look wonderful – you could have, for instance, a round table on one side and a small chest on the other. This breaks up the perfection of having everything matching and creates a little bit of the unexpected style I think works so well. Sometimes people are concerned about the varying heights of mismatched pieces when a bedside lamp is placed on top of them. Personally, I love this look, but if you have an absolute aversion to it, I suggest propping up the lower bedside lamp with a few books or magazines to the same height as the lamp sitting on the opposite side of the bed.

Obviously the amount of room you have in your bedroom dictates your final choice of bedside furniture. If you have a lot of space beside your bed, consider using an antique commode or chest of drawers or, as I have done in our bedroom, on my side I have an antique bureau as I tend to do a lot of work in bed at night and need somewhere to store my paperwork, magazines, books, diary and notepad. Brad has a very small old Georgian table on his side with just enough room for his alarm clock and bedside lamp. I love the difference in scale, as it means we each have a piece reflective of our needs. Before making a decision, ask yourself what you tend to use your bedside table for. Some people read in bed, so need enough space and storage for their books, lamps, clocks and other bits and pieces. Others just need a surface for their watch and not much else.

- BEDSIDE LAMPS -

People often make the mistake of going for small bedside lamps. Large, tall bedside lamps are a much better option – the light they give is more suitable for reading in bed, and they look much more balanced when placed next to a high bedhead. Beds are higher these days, so taller bedside lamps should be used to compensate for that. Wall lights provide an alternative option for task lighting for reading in bed and can allow for less clutter on your bedside table. I prefer the use of table lamps for the look and style they can add to a room.

*I'm definitely
a fan of upholstered bedheads.
They're soft and luxurious
to lean against while
reading in bed.*

- QUILTS & LINEN -

The use of a beautiful white French quilt on a bed is something
I never get tired of. Its simple, crisp and pretty quilted characteristics
provide a wonderful and flexible backdrop for the other decorative
items in the room. An array of patterned cushions can be placed
on a white bedspread and can be changed as you wish because of the
flexibility the white provides. Washing French quilts is much easier
and less expensive than having to send them off to the drycleaner.
White bed linen is like sleeping in a soft, floating cloud.

To layer up your bedroom and create interest, consider placing
a textile such as a vintage suzani or a colourful kantha quilt along the
base of your bed on top of the white quilt. This not only adds texture,
but can bring another colourful element into the room.

{ THE BATHROOM }

Small pieces of antique furniture look lovely in bathrooms. They add an element of cosiness, and interest and personality to a room that we usually don't think about furnishing. Whether it's a small table to place some towels on and a beautiful tray with lots of perfume and lotion for your guests, or a lovely old chair upholstered in a pretty fabric, it's a great look that is both beautiful and practical. When placing an upholstered piece in a bathroom, whether it is a small chair or stool, use an exterior-grade fabric as its durability and mould resistance ensures longevity and sustainability.

{ THE VERANDAH }

Here in Queensland, we live on our verandahs in the summer. Verandah rooms can be a beautiful addition to your home, and there's nothing better than furnishing them in a similar way to the interior lounge room. If your verandah space is covered and protected from the elements, why not consider having cane furniture covered in beautiful outdoor fabrics, as well as lamps with shades made in exterior fabrics? Verandah rooms are wonderful places to entertain, so consider making them as comfortable and as attractive as possible. Even though it is much firmer to sit on than ordinary foam, use marine-grade foam on furniture made for exterior spaces as it will last much longer in the elements than ordinary foam. And always use exterior-grade paint to paint any of the furniture.

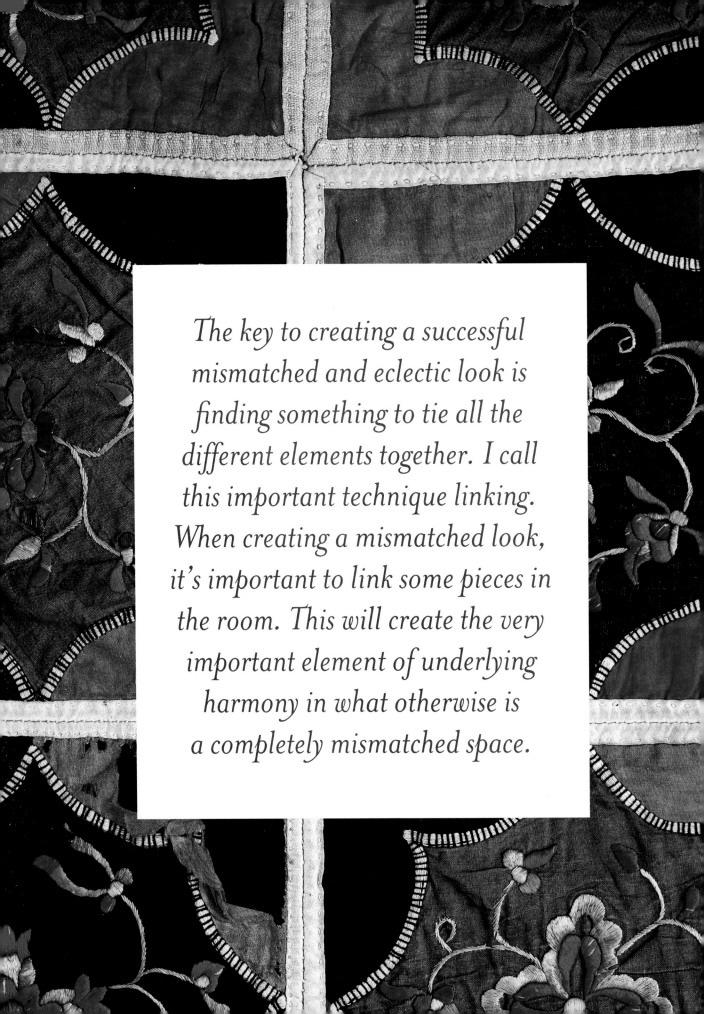

The key to creating a successful mismatched and eclectic look is finding something to tie all the different elements together. I call this important technique linking. When creating a mismatched look, it's important to link some pieces in the room. This will create the very important element of underlying harmony in what otherwise is a completely mismatched space.

It's all in the mix not the match

I have talked about all the ingredients required to create a magical home, but it's very important to know that no matter what pieces you have, be they antique or modern, cheap or expensive, heirloom or new, it's all in the way you mix and layer the different things you love and have collected over time. It's all in the mix, not the match!

Your collection should be created by the love of particular objects and pieces, not whether or not they are going to match or be in fashion. Pulling together a variety of furniture styles, fabrics and objects in a haphazard arrangement is paramount to creating a home that has soul and style. It's important not to make any one style dominate in your space. Keep a balanced mix by introducing lots of different pieces from different eras, different places. By bringing together these sometimes clashing things, there's less chance of the look dating and becoming old and uninteresting. The end result is a look that is completely special and one that will grow and change as your own life grows and changes.

It's much easier to keep a mismatched space evolving than it is for a perfectly contrived and inside-the-box space. The most successful rooms are those that are clashing, layered and imperfect and are not of any particular style you could ever describe. These rooms are unique to their owners and admired by everyone who steps inside them. They are the rooms we should all endeavour to live in because they truly reflect the lives of the people who own them. With the right mix, nobody will be able to distinguish between what was cheap and what was expensive. Isn't that a wonderful thing to be able to create; to me, it's a sign of true style.

part 04

....

{ RESOURCES }

I've always loved books.
Here are some I refer to constantly,
along with some of my favourite newer
sources of design inspiration.

- BOOKS -

Not only do books provide excellent reference material, they are beautiful objects to display. Nothing looks more inviting than a coffee table or ottoman filled with stacks of books. Except, maybe, piles of books stored under sofa tables, hall tables and console tables on the floor at varying – almost disarrayed – heights. For the ultimate in book display, built-in floor-to-ceiling bookcases not only give abundant storage, they give a house much sought-after, lived-in atmosphere. A wall full of colourful book spines can give a room so much fabulous, layered colour. So, too, can bookcases filled with a few treasured objects placed here and there amongst the mix, but it's always advisable to have more books than bits so that it doesn't become too busy and bitsy!

I guarantee you will underestimate how many books you will need to fill your bookcase. A few years ago, we had a beautiful custom-built bookcase installed into a home in the country. I arrived at the house to arrange the bookcase and found five boxes of books. I told my client we would need at least another fifteen boxes and she didn't believe me, until we filled only a quarter of the shelves. Over the next few months she collected enough books to completely fill the cabinet.

I often refer to old design books and even old magazines for inspiration and ideas. I particularly love old design and decoration books that show how people lived at that particular time. I am always excited to discover different details and furniture styles in old books and try to work out how I can bring them back to life in my work. By referencing old-fashioned ideas and styles such as sofa shapes, curtain details and bedhead designs, and then adding a layer of newness by the choice of fabric or by mixing in a couple of modern pieces of furniture, you can create a very interesting look that refers to the past yet suits the way we live today.

THE LANGUAGE OF FLOWERS ✽ MANDY KIRKBY

ANDREW MARTIN INTERIOR DESIGN REVIEW VOLUME 14 ANDREW MARTIN INTERNATIONAL

PRIVATE SYDNEY RETHMEIER • REED BURNS

DECORATING WITH FABRIC LIBERTY STYLE CHARMIAN WATKINS DOUBLEDAY

CONVERSATIONS with CREATIVE WOMEN {VOLUME TWO}

WILLIAM YEOWARD AT HOME CICO BOOKS

Australians at Home
TERENCE LANE & JESSIE SERLE
A DOCUMENTARY HISTORY OF AUSTRALIAN DOMESTIC INTERIORS OXFORD

BUNNY WILLIAMS AN AFFAIR WITH A HOUSE stewart tabori & chang

OBERTO GILI HOME SWEET HOME R

HABITUALLY CHIC Creativity at Work HEATHER CLAWSON

Yves Saint Laurent
David Teboul
Éditions de La Martinière

TERENCE CONRAN STAFFORD CLIFF INSPIRATION

THE WAY HOME Jeffrey Bilhuber R

ENGLISH DECORATION Ben Pentreath

KATZ *Pleasure Palaces*
The ART & HOMES of HUNT SLONEM pH

David Hicks on decoration – with.fabrics    World Publishing

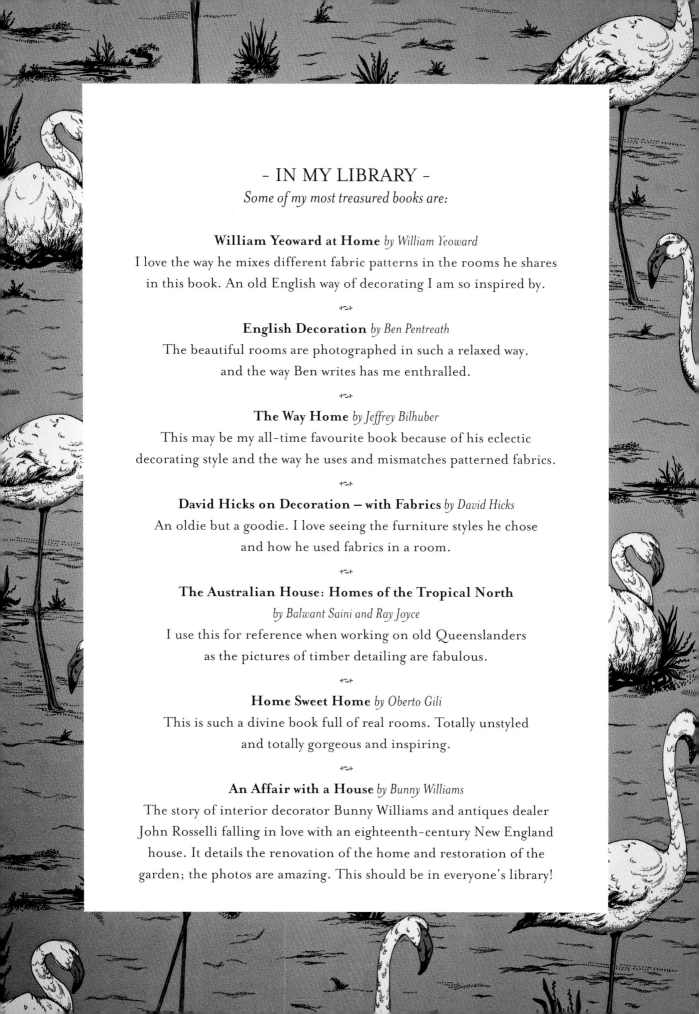

- IN MY LIBRARY -

Some of my most treasured books are:

William Yeoward at Home *by William Yeoward*
I love the way he mixes different fabric patterns in the rooms he shares
in this book. An old English way of decorating I am so inspired by.

✦

English Decoration *by Ben Pentreath*
The beautiful rooms are photographed in such a relaxed way,
and the way Ben writes has me enthralled.

✦

The Way Home *by Jeffrey Bilhuber*
This may be my all-time favourite book because of his eclectic
decorating style and the way he uses and mismatches patterned fabrics.

✦

David Hicks on Decoration – with Fabrics *by David Hicks*
An oldie but a goodie. I love seeing the furniture styles he chose
and how he used fabrics in a room.

✦

The Australian House: Homes of the Tropical North
by Balwant Saini and Ray Joyce
I use this for reference when working on old Queenslanders
as the pictures of timber detailing are fabulous.

✦

Home Sweet Home *by Oberto Gili*
This is such a divine book full of real rooms. Totally unstyled
and totally gorgeous and inspiring.

✦

An Affair with a House *by Bunny Williams*
The story of interior decorator Bunny Williams and antiques dealer
John Rosselli falling in love with an eighteenth-century New England
house. It details the renovation of the home and restoration of the
garden; the photos are amazing. This should be in everyone's library!

- BLOGS -

Some of my all time favourite blogs are:

Ben Pentreath

Like his beautiful book, the images Ben shares of his divine parsonage
and garden at Dorset are breathtaking and his witty writing makes me
smile. He is honest and informative, quirky and positively charming.

❦

Style Court

This continues to be a wonderful source of inspiration. Courtney
Barnes is extremely passionate about decoration and design, and her
knowledge is outstanding. She is also humble and supportive and
I am forever indebted to her for connecting with me when I first
started blogging.

❦

The Design Files

Lucy writes about creative, talented Australians. Her support of up-
and-coming artists and designers is wonderful for everyone. Her blog
has become a fabulous resource for the design industry in Australia.

❦

decor8

Holly's was one of the first design blogs and continues to be a fabulous
resource. She supports crafters, makers, designers and artists from all
over the world, and has been a generous supporter of mine over the
years. I thank her for all the lovely posts she has written on her
world-famous blog.

❦

Habitually Chic

Heather is so uptown chic! Living a fabulous life in NYC, Heather
gets some fantastic insights into the lives of designers, and is invited
to the chicest of NYC events, all of which she shares on her blog.
I also love following her on Instagram, and it was wonderful meeting
her at Crosby Street Hotel in New York a couple of years ago.
She is a treasure!

- INSTAGRAM -

Instagram is so quick and a lot less work than blogging. I follow lots of creative people and find handmade products for my work this way. I share pictures of my life as a designer on my feed; it's a great way of showing my work and ideas to my followers and clients.

Some of my all time favourite instagrammers are:

@aerin
I love Aerin Lauder's photos of her grandmother's house
in the Hamptons and her glamorous life.

@amandacbrooks
Amanda posts photos of her stylish life and lots of garden and
countryside inspiration.

@butterland
Photos posted of the divine Newstead Butter Factory where Greg
Hatton and Katie Marx live.

@waynepate
I love Wayne's style. He's an artist who lives in Brooklyn, New York.
He posts beautiful photos of his life and work.

@katiemarxflowers
This very clever and inspiring florist posts beautiful images of her
arrangements and snippets of her life.

@roopapemmaraju
Australian fashion designer Roopa Pemmaraju posts photos of the
outfits she makes using Aboriginal designed fabrics. Very inspiring.

@ingridweir
Designer Ingrid Weir posts images of her gypsy life full of creativity
and travel.

-CREDITS-

Details of artists and fabrics

COVER illustration by Pip Boydell (of Quadrille Jacaranda fabric) PAGE i artwork by David Rankin, PAGE 3 lampshade fabric by Pigott's Store, PAGE 10 main artwork by Karlee Rawkins, top row right artwork by Adrian Lockhart, second row left artwork by Maureen Hansen, second row right artwork by Adam Lester, bottom row middle artwork by Sacha Dobinson-Yates, bottom row right artwork by Harry Lipke, PAGE 16 yellow fabric Pondicherry by Katherine Rally, PAGE 19 artwork by Bridgette McNab; fabric Ralph Lauren Paisley, PAGE 35 artwork by Ann Curlewis, PAGE 42 fabric on chair GP & J Baker Hydrangea Bird, lampshade fabric David Hicks Diamond Geometric, PAGE 55 artwork by Sam Fullbrook, PAGE 62 artwork by David Bromley, PAGE 63 fabric David Hicks Ditsy Floral, PAGE 64 fabric Manuel Canovas Serendip, PAGE 65 top artwork by Ena Gibson, bottom artwork by Dianne Robinson PAGE 67 artwork by David Bromley, PAGE 68 artwork by Lisa Harris, PAGE 71 artwork by Julian Meagher, PAGE 80 artwork by Adam Lester, PAGE 85 artwork by David Bromley, PAGE 86 artwork with circular motif by Rachel Castle, middle left and lower left artwork by Harry Lipke, PAGE 91 artwork by Ken Brinsmead, PAGE 94 wallpaper Designers Guild Amalienborg, PAGE 103 artwork by Karlee Rawkins; yellow cushion fabric Manuel Canovas Serendip, PAGE 117 artwork by Ian Smith; sofa fabric Kathryn Ireland Safi Suzani, PAGE 123 fabric GP & J Baker Magnolia, PAGE 125 pink cushion fabric Quadrille Aquarius, artwork by Utopia artist, NT, PAGE 127 clockwise from top left, vintage artwork, artwork by Adam Lester, Sacha Dobinson-Yates, Harry Lipke, PAGE 130 lampshade fabric Manuel Canovas Serendip, PAGE 132 bottom right artwork by Bridgette McNab, PAGE 134–35 artwork by Sally Gabori; wallpaper Anna Spiro for Porter's Paints Round and Round the Garden, PAGE 137 artwork of single flower in jam jar by Polly Jones, shell artwork by Pip Boydell, artwork of blue and yellow flowers by Diana Favell, PAGE 138–39 girl skipping and boy reading artworks by David Bromley, PAGE 144 artwork by D. Featherstone, PAGE 152 ships artwork by David Bromley, PAGE 156-57 top middle artwork by Pip Boydell, PAGE 159 artwork by Geoffrey Pound, PAGE 161 artwork by Sally Stokes, PAGE 167 main artwork by Richard Dunlop, top two left artworks by Nadine Sawyer, top far right artwork by Hilary Herrmann, centre of middle row artwork by Pip Boydell, small colourful artwork in middle row right Gemma Smith, PAGE 168–69 artwork by Marina Strocchi, PAGE 170 artwork by Emily Kame Kngwarreye, PAGE 173 wallpaper Anna Spiro for Porter's Paints Round and Round the Garden, PAGE 174 top row artwork by Pip Boydell, PAGE 178 small artwork above lamp by Bridgette McNab, yellow artwork by Linda Sheppard, PAGE 184–85 small artworks on right by Judith Sinnamon, artwork on wall at right by Jessica Geron, PAGE 187 artwork by Matthew Johnson; lampshade fabric Kathryn Ireland Safi Suzani, cushion fabric Manuel Canovas Beauregard, PAGE 188 artwork by David Rankin, PAGE 190 top row left and middle row left artworks by Harry Lipke, PAGE 192 left artwork by Robert Malherbe, right artwork by David Bromley, PAGE 200 artwork on left wall by Sally Gabori, artwork on bookcase by Maureen Hansen; wallpaper Anna Spiro for Porter's Paints Round and Round the Garden, PAGE 207 wallpaper Cole & Son Flamingo.

LAUREN AND HIS WIFE, RICKY
OPPOSITE, FROM TOP: A FAMILY
BOATING EXCURSION; THE
YACHTLIKE WHITE DECK

arded the entrance to a temple that crumbled long ago but
med to welcome us to the oasis where Sand Castle stands.
use is built of mud, in the traditional 5,000-year-old manner.
all is a play of light and shadow. You enter through a faded
wooden door, following a corridor to a large square
rd. Off it sits the grand living and dining room, with its long
can tile table, narghile (water pipe), and colours and comforts
f an orientalist painting. Adjacent is the kitchen, sacred

domain of Ashraf, the cook, who would later delight my palate with
eggplant salad, chicken with caramelised orange, and a wonderful
soup using mallow leaves, called mouloukhia. Stepping out into the
courtyard, I noticed a remarkable thing: a huge fireplace that
transforms the space into a room open to the sky. It is the centre and
soul of the house.
We climbed to the second floor, where Louboutin very
graciously gave me his room, the master bedroom. There's a low ►

FAVOURITE
THINGS

wonder

A QUIET
Stella McCartney co
blend dress, $4,350,
from a selection at
Robby Ingham. Chanel
stretch jersey swimsuit,
$1,350, and beach
towel, $950, from the
Chanel boutiques.

Lisa Blonde, wearing
Chanel, in the living room
of her London home.
The 'angel' photograph
by Craig McDean of a ba
enpire on the wall behind
was a wedding gift.

PORTER'S
PAINTS

RED GERBER

VOYAGE   CHIN

©Copyright Porter's Paints Pty Ltd   ©Copyright Porter's Paints Pty Ltd   47

HOROSCOP
Words: Jessica Adams

TAURUS APR 21 – MAY 21
Your chances of straightforward business or
property results are much higher in June, as
May is one of those months when done deals
come unstuck and any communication or
technical errors get in the way of firm outcomes.
You may think you've found a new direction
near the 24th, but it may not be until the second
half of June that everything falls into place. What
happens near the 8th finds you dealing with the
reality of your partnership, a former soul mate,

VIRGO AUG 24 – SEP 22
In May, you will want to receive a f
from your boss, client or colleagu
professional issue. Try to be patie
not be until June that you know wh
stand. If paperwork is involved in t
read the fine print. The world of pap
internet or travel will also be on you
you should also allow for complica
is a testing ground. You will be ab
wider view of your daily workload, y

Acknowledgements

I didn't know how much work it would be to produce a book; thanks from the bottom of my heart to everyone who worked so hard to make it happen. I am so thankful to Kirsten Abbott whose idea it was, and to the fabulous Julie Gibbs for taking me under her wing and into the wonderful world of Lantern. Katrina O'Brien, thank you for all your organising and understanding during those stressful days. Leta Keens and Tracy Lines — you girls are amazing. I felt so safe and under control in your care. Thank you for making my book something to be proud of. Felix Forest, thank you for all your time and hard work. Sharyn Cairns, you took my things and turned them into photos I could only dream of. Thank you for your incredible work, super energy and enthusiasm. Lara Hutton, thank you for helping make those last round of photos so perfectly me. Jared Fowler, thank you for making the time to photograph me. I loathe having my photo taken and you did a beautiful job. Vanessa Colyer Tay — you were so lovely to me. I can't believe you brought that humongous box of flowers from Sydney! Thank you for everything you helped create. Pip Spiro (at the time of writing, she was Pip Boydell but is now my sister-in-law), I can't thank you enough for the hours you poured into painting the cover in the middle of planning your wedding. I am forever inspired by you and your amazing creativity. Thank you, sister! Thank you to the suppliers for lending me props — Jen from Vintage Finds, Les from Marburg Antiques, the always fabulous Morrison Polkinghorne, Space Furniture and Sue from Vieille Branche. Thank you, Robyn, Peter and Kerrie for making the things we needed at such short notice. What would we do without you!

CONVERSATIONS with CREATIVE WOMEN [VOLUME TWO]

CONVE
with
C

(v

by Tess McCabe

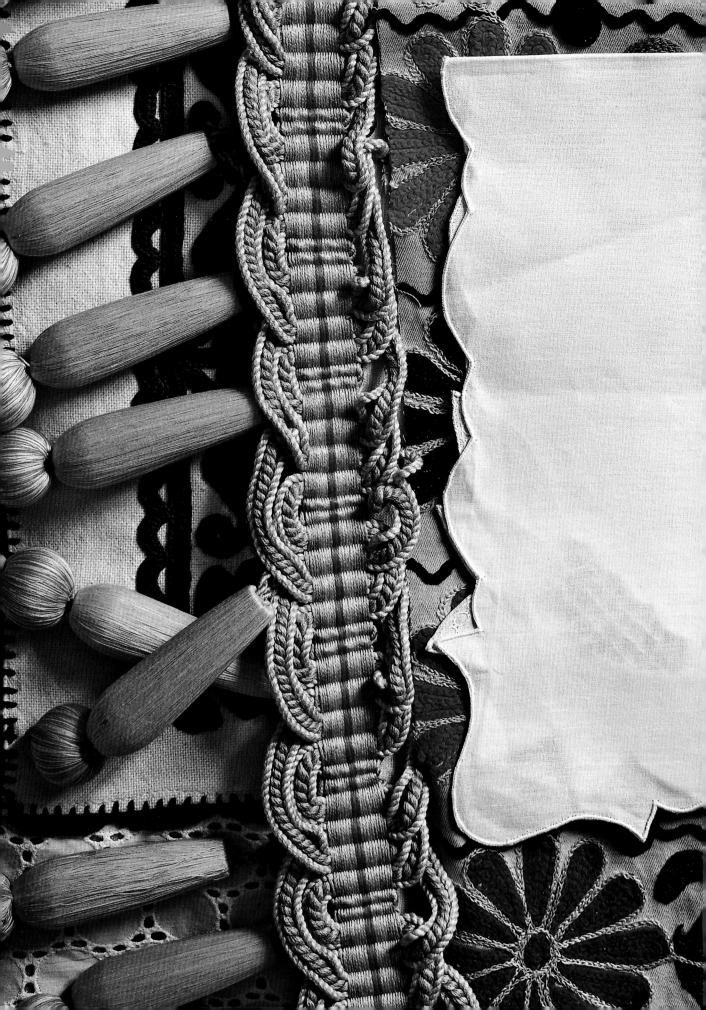

Troy, my upholsterer, thank you for allowing us to photograph your work space, and for all you do. And a heartfelt thank you to Ellen Newman for getting me started on the book. Huge thanks to my cousin Ben Young for reading my manuscript when nobody else wanted a bar of it. You are so clever and generous and I love you so much. Kelly Polkinghorne, you are one of my closest and dearest friends and I thank you with everything I have for sticking by me all these years and for sorting out that wretched manuscript when I didn't know where to turn. You are a friend who everyone wants to have yet only a few are so lucky to have. Sarah and Olivia, you are the best girls anyone could hope to work with. Thank you for all you have done for me, and for all you did to help with this book. You inspire me every day and I love coming to work with you two fabulous chicks! Michelle, you are the best. Thank you for everything. You have made my life so much better! Mum and Dad, thank you for everything and for listening during our late-night phone chats. You always set me straight. Rhonda and Stacey, thank you for making our house beautiful and clean all the time and for starting early those many days of photography. Merv, thank you for being my garden friend and for making the garden wonderful for the photos. Thank you Barry and Joyce for the home-grown produce. You are so generous. Thank you to my ninety-eight-year-old grandmother for having us photograph your house too many times. Thank you to my grandmother Lel for having us photograph you and your treasured things. To Brad, gosh, thank you for putting up with my tears and stress and for constantly trying to keep me amused. You are a wonderful husband and my very best friend. I love you so much. Max and Harry, thank you for putting up with having such a busy and, at times, tired and grumpy Mum. I love you both so much. A big thank you to all my blog readers, Instagram followers and supporters. I wouldn't be here today without your encouragement and interest. Last but not least, thank you to all my wonderful clients for allowing me to photograph the rooms we have created together. Without you, this book would never have been possible. I love you all so much. You are the best clients in the world and I am so grateful that you ask me to help you create beautiful things in your beautiful homes. Where would I be without you?!?!

Lots of love,

Anna

xxx

An Hachette UK company
www.hachette.co.uk

First published in Australia by Penguin Group (Australia) in 2014

This edition published in Great Britain in 2015 by
Conran Octopus Ltd, a division of Octopus Publishing Group Ltd
Carmelite House
50 Victoria Embankment
London EC4Y 0DZ
www.octopusbooks.co.uk
www.octopusbooksusa.com

Distributed in the US by
Hachette Book Group
1290 Avenue of the Americas
4th and 5th Floors
New York, NY 10020

Distributed in Canada by
Canadian Manda Group
664 Annette St.
Toronto, Ontario, Canada M6S 2C8

ISBN 978 1 84091 693 5

A CIP catalogue record for this book is available from the British Library.

Printed and bound in China

10 9 8 7 6 5 4 3

Design and art direction by Tracy Lines @ TLC © Penguin Group (Australia)
Cover artwork by Pip Boydell of Quadrille 'Jacaranda' fabric (quadrillefabrics.com)
Reprinted by kind permission of Quadrille and the artist
Photography by Sharyn Cairns
Except for pages iv, 42, 54, 55, 64, 72–73, 83, 87, 88, 102, 123, 156–157, 163, 168–169, 170, 173,
178, 181, 183, 184–185, 187, 195, 200, 210 by Felix Forest and pages 114–115 by Lantern Studio
Author photograph opposite page 1 by Jared Fowler

Typeset in Mrs Eaves by Tracy Lines @ TLC
Colour separation by Splitting Image Colour Studio, Clayton, Victoria, Australia

The Woodblock Painting of CRESSIDA CAMPBELL

CRISS CANNING THE PURSUIT OF BEAUTY   DAVID THOMAS

I LOVE the summer wind GOMA on a Monday scalloped ed
hope French blue patchwork torn edges rips and holes broa
faded blue linen Old Staffordshire dogs Harry blue hydrange
chipped old furniture denim bows fringing frills parquetry and
box pleating old silk scarves raffia Max sleeping in collecting
batik table lamps floor lamps wall lamps block-printed any
Deco mirrors old battery vases things children make seersuck
driving in the country fireplaces pale pink walls Frank Sina
in concrete houses Neddie treasure hunting surprises birthd
checks and stripes New York in winter trophies lemons with
holidays pink blue white yellow orange green pottery strawb
silk singing in the car open windows beach walks Belgian line
frangipani at Christmas Fridays old botanical prints manner
canvas ticking appliqué generosity the first poppies slipcove
pinboards tearsheets and old magazines revisited painted flo
markets really big windows old bamboo wall hooks blanket
November flats loyalty smiles and laughs seagrass matting
apologies hand-written notes acceptance vintage braid Fren
notebooks phone calls with Mum remembering mementoes th